THE LAS VEGAS MASSACRE
CONNECTIONS

FINDING STRENGTH THROUGH TRAGEDY AFTER AMERICA'S DEADLIEST MASS SHOOTING

MARK GRAY

WITH CONTRIBUTIONS FROM MARY JO VON TILLOW

WILDBLUE
PRESS

WildBluePress.com

The Las Vegas Massacre Connections published by:
WILDBLUE PRESS
P.O. Box 102440
Denver, Colorado 80250

WILDBLUE PRESS is registered at the U.S. Patent and Trademark Offices.

ISBN 978-1-964730-84-4 Hardcover
ISBN 978-1-964730-85-1 Trade Paperback
ISBN 978-1-964730-83-7 eBook
Cover design © 2025 WildBlue Press. All rights reserved.

Interior Formatting and Book Cover Design by Elijah Toten
www.totencreative.com

THE LAS VEGAS MASSACRE
CONNECTIONS

DEDICATION

For Kurt von Tillow, Denise Burditus, Paulette Dion, Derrick Fudge, Bryan Gray and the families of the 58.

INTRODUCTION

"I don't want to move on, but I do want to move forward."

Those are the words of Mary Jo von Tillow. For four straight years in the early fall, the von Tillow family descended on Las Vegas to attend the Route 91 Harvest Festival, a three-day country music concert showcasing the genre's biggest names. Over the years, performers included Miranda Lambert, Toby Keith, Luke Bryan, Blake Shelton, Eric Church, Morgan Wallen and Tim McGraw.

The annual festival was a non-negotiable venture for Kurt and Mary Jo von Tillow: they were going no matter who was headlining.

Sadly, the 2017 version of the festival was the last one they ever attended. At 10:05 p.m., a gunman (who is not named in this book) opened fire on the concert venue from his 32nd-floor hotel suite at Mandalay Bay, a ritzy hotel adjacent to the concert grounds, which was filled with 22,000 country music fans. In that instance, every single person was in real danger of being shot and killed, including Jason Aldean, who was just four songs into his expected 90-minute set. Everyone was highly exposed to the shooter, who had an elevated position and an extensive arsenal. After the massacre, investigators recovered 1,057 shell casings in the adjoining Mandalay Bay hotel rooms. There's no way of truly knowing the first victim of that event, but it's feasible that terrible honor could go to Kurt von Tillow. He was shot and fatally wounded while Aldean was still singing.

Mary Jo, of course, went through all the stages of grief, but there's no playbook for "husband dies in the largest mass shooting in U.S. history." Sometimes, she wanted to detach herself from all she knew and become a hermit, but that's not her style.

Determined to find a silver lining in the tragic death of her husband, Mary Jo began meeting other Route 91 victims and people who wanted to help. She chose to live and seek out the good (and the good people) that came into her life because of Oct. 1, 2017. Her correspondence wasn't limited to just victims who experienced Route 91, but also to people who experienced their own loss. Before she knew it, she had developed deep friendships with other survivors. This is a book of their stories as much as Mary Jo's.

Laid out chapter by chapter, Tragic Connections biographizes Mary Jo's newly built, tragically built inner circle. She is the single thread linking all the individual stories, but, similar to a Quentin Tarantino movie, many of the stories and people chronicled overlap.

Tragic Connections is not a book of sorrow but rather a different way of looking at the effects of tragedy and overcoming them. Much light can be found during the darkest times.

Had that 2017 evening not happened, Mary Jo would have never met Tommy Maher, a Long Island fire commissioner who travels the country in a van doing random acts of kindness on his own dime. Tommy's inspiration came after his best friend, a fellow firefighter, died in the 9/11 attacks.

Had that 2017 evening not happened, Mary Jo would have never met Jeff Dion, a lawyer who got statute of limitations laws changed to allow sexual assault victims to go after their abusers (the legal change sent shockwaves through the Catholic Church and Boy Scouts of America). One of the most prominent victims' rights advocates in the country,

Jeff's inspiration came after a serial killer murdered his sister, the same killer murdered Adam Walsh, the son of America's Most Wanted Host, John Walsh.

Had that 2017 evening not happened, Mary Jo would have never met Tony Burditus, a former Army Special Forces officer who did some of America's most secretive work overseas in war zones. Like Mary Jo, Tony's wife was also shot on Oct. 1, 2017.

Had that 2017 evening not happened, Mary Jo would have never met Lindsay Lawler, a country music singer/songwriter who had her wedding during a state of emergency in Texas. Lindsay, an advocate for the trucking industry, has performed at Arlington National Cemetery, the United States Capitol, and the famed Tootsies bar in Nashville.

Had that 2017 evening not happened, Mary Jo never would have met Dion Green, a Dayton, Ohio, native who lost his father in the 2019 Oregon District shooting. Dion's life reads like a "Scared Straight" documentary: he served eight years in prison for drug dealing, having been charged under the RICO law. He's been kidnapped, and a string of deadly tornadoes flattened his house. His life has now turned around; he advocates for gun reform and has created a foundation for at-risk youths.

Had that 2017 evening not happened, Mary Jo and Mark Gray would never have come together for this book. Gray is also a survivor of Route 91, as he was there that evening covering the festival for Rolling Stone.

All of the subjects documented have dealt with their trauma in some capacity, but they all have inspiring stories of pushing forward despite the tragic hands they've been dealt.

Over the course of two years, Gray spoke with every subject in this book multiple times via phone, FaceTime, email and several in-person visits in Las Vegas. He also pored over media coverage and books pertaining to each individual and scoured their social media outlets. Regarding the Las Vegas shooting specifically, he spent days reading over the Federal Emergency Management Agency's 61-page "1 October After-Action Report" and the 187-page "LVMPD Criminal Investigative Report of the 1 October Mass Casualty Shooting" to confirm timing, shooting location, festival layout and bullet casings dispensed.

CHAPTER 1

Warm blood covered her hands, clothes and skin, but none of it was hers. Around her were others whose lives were unexpectedly bloodstained. The overhead soundtrack wasn't that of music, but instead of rhythmic explosions, panicked screaming and thousands of shoes galloping on the pavement, almost as if they were an elephant stampede. The 15-acre area on the South Las Vegas Strip was illuminated by large floodlights, providing clear vision to combat the darkness that had already fallen over the evening. Those same lights also allowed her to see the result of the diabolical darkness of one man's heart and his constantly twitching trigger finger.

The largest mass shooting in United States history was only just beginning, but Mary Jo von Tillow's world had already stopped spinning on its axis.

Mary Jo von Tillow

Oct. 1, 2017: Morning

The morning her husband was murdered in cold blood, along with 57 others, began like a typical fall Sunday, full of food, football and family. Morning would later become mourning after a searing bullet found a home in his once-beating heart.

Naturally, Mary Jo von Tillow, the fair-haired, hazel-eyed, ever-devoted wife, never could have seen this coming after a fun, profitable weekend in Las Vegas.

Alongside her beloved husband, Kurt von Tillow, and a handful of family members, Mary Jo and the group spent Friday and Saturday at the Route 91 Harvest Festival, checking out artists like Maren Morris, Eric Church, Sam Hunt and Lee Brice perform. A three-day country music festival on the Vegas Strip, Route 91, as most called it, began in 2014 and was an instant success. For 72 hours, fans would gather to listen to headliners or up-and-comers; they'd shop at merchandise stands on the 15-acre blacktop lot and support the local economy via copious amounts of whisky and light beer. It was equivalent to a giant outdoor honkey tonk — a true country musical festival focused on the music, not social media influencers.

A smaller stage toward the back of the grounds called "Next From Nashville" featured up-and-coming acts that hadn't quite gained main stage prominence yet. Sitting under an open-air white tent, that stage was just past the never-ending row of food trucks shilling every cuisine imaginable. Wallen, Luke Combs, Midland and Ashley McBryde played there in 2017.

The von Tillows, in one form or another, had attended the Route 91 festival every year since its inception and lived it up.

Come Sunday, the deliriously content group woke up in their Caesars Palace room a little groggy and slightly hungover.

"I'm feeling last night," Mary Jo freely admitted to her husband while rubbing her eyes in the king-size bed, the sun creeping into the room via a crack in the blackout curtains.

Following a quick meal to restore life, Kurt and Mary Jo took their magnetic smiles to the hotel's popular Sports Book. Their daughter, Jessica, and her then-husband, CJ, joined her parents to gamble and watch the NFL games on the massive LED screens that even Iron Man would be jealous of. Kurt's sister Dee Ann Hyatt and her daughter, Araina Hyatt, eventually got in on the action, too, and they all bested the house, winning bets on the 49ers, Steelers, Rams and Jets.

They won big and felt rejuvenated. Huge winnings can have that effect.

By the time Team von Tillow headed to the music festival grounds following the afternoon slate of games, the group was unassumingly walking around with a significant sum in their collective pockets.

Oct. 1, 2017: 5 p.m.

The distance between Caesars Palace and the Las Vegas Village, where the festival took place, was just over two miles. Mary Jo and Kurt and their small entourage arrived shortly before dusk and headed straight to their usual spot, where a vast swath of green, faux turf meets the blacktop on the far west side of the venue. They'd stood in this spot, about 20 yards from the stage and next to a VIP tent, so often over the years that there should have been placeholders.

"Reserved For The von Tillows."

Despite it being October, the Vegas heat was unrelenting, as it was still 90 degrees outside. Aside from the fortunate few with access to shade, the crowd was getting cooked. People standing directly on the blacktop must have felt like they were standing on a Benihana hibachi grill.

Knowing they had an early morning flight on Monday back to Sacramento, Mary Jo, Kurt, etc., all decided it was best to limit their alcohol intake—just a couple of Coors Lights to wet their whistles. While the idea sounded well-thought-out (and A for effort), the execution of sobriety wasn't going according to plan.

At 7:30 p.m., country duo Big & Rich ended their set, and the temperature dropped. It got harshly cold, especially by Vegas standards. Between the time the family arrived and the set ended, the temperature had fallen 23 degrees. It was thermometer whiplash. Kurt, however, was just getting warmed up.

"Change our flights," he blurted to his wife, a silver Coors Light in hand. "We're not leaving at six in the morning."

"Kurt, oh my God, I told you a month ago we shouldn't get the 6 a.m. flight in the first place!"

Turning her head to hide her annoyed eye roll, she reached into her purse to grab her iPhone to begin searching for alternative flights out of McCarran Airport. In some capacity, Mary Jo knew damn well this would happen because this kind of thing always happened! They should have booked that 8:35 a.m. flight back home to Northern California to begin with.

After Jake Owen's 75-minute set on the main stage, the crowd, buzzing with excitement, waited for Jason Aldean, the night's headliner and the culminating act of the three-day festival. Jason was also a headliner at the first Route 91 festival in 2014, so they were confident he'd put on a hell of a show, and he did for three songs.

During Aldean's fourth song, "When She Says Baby," a loud, incessant popping noise saturated the area.

January 1983

She had to get to Filthy McNasty's early for the Chippendales — that's how Mary Jo's love story with Kurt started.

Her sister Kim and a friend were supposed to join Mary Jo at the beer-soaked dive bar in North Hollywood that night, but Kim got sick. Still, MJ — as she would later be known — was in her 20s and wasn't about to miss a bunch of tan, fit, bare-torso-ed men in too much baby oil hand out lap dances and do pearl-clutching stripteases. Back then, Filthy McNasty's — what everyone called it despite actually being named FM Station — was essentially ladies' night from 7 pm to 10 pm. That's when the men wearing little more than bow ties and shirt cuffs performed, grinded up on women, chairs and greased silver poles. Then, after the women were all hot and bothered, the men would saunter into the bar, trying to get lucky.

That 1983 evening was the night MJ met Kurt von Tillow. Naturally, Kurt will tell you that he was one of the physically fit Chippendales, but that would be a hilarious exaggeration. It's not that Kurt was out of shape — he wasn't — but his gym routine consisted of six-inch curls with a cold beer in his right hand.

Filthy McNasty's, or FM, wasn't just your average bar in the San Fernando Valley. It really was the premier live music space in the '80s. Bands like Audioslave, Soundgarden and Train all performed there in their early years. The venue helped launch the careers of a bevy of '80s hair bands like Warrant and Poison. The bar, albeit in a different location, was glamorized forty years later on Amazon Prime's "Daisy Jones & The Six." The miniseries even starred actress Riley Keough, the granddaughter of Elvis Presley. Perhaps it isn't a coincidence, but Elvis often frequented the Filthy McNasty's on the Sunset Strip in Los Angeles. Before FM's doors eventually closed in 1997, rock stars would often hang out there because they felt comfortable enough to drink, smoke pot or snort cocaine openly without fear of being judged or photographed. Think of it like a speakeasy, but everyone was welcome. Still, it was very much a what-happens-here-stays-here type of place. Thank God social media wasn't around at that time.

On this particular evening, MJ was the biggest rockstar there in Kurt's eyes, but she most certainly did not reciprocate that… at least not yet. As a single woman, she was casually dating a few different guys. Kurt, though, was doing his best to make a great first impression. Dressed in his finest wrinkled long-sleeve shirt and clean jeans, he offered to buy drinks for the woman he couldn't take his eyes off of. In their conversations, it wasn't that he was guarded but rather that he was genuinely interested in Mary Jo. When he did get personal, Kurt often spoke of his mother, Joanne, and sister, Dee Ann. Kurt's eyes lit up with pride when he talked about the two central women in his life, but he would always steer the conversation back to Mary Jo. His compliments were cheesy but seemed legitimately heartfelt.

"Mary Jo, you're beautiful," he would say as cigarette smoke wafted through the air like a tobacco tornado. The endearing compliments continued. The focus of his eyes proved that he meant everything he said, too.

Persistent as ever, Kurt asked for MJ's phone number, and she happily gave it to him, especially given that he was "playing the field" at the moment. While she assumed she'd just add him to the stable of men in her Rolodex, he felt something else.

The smitten Kurt and an intrigued MJ went their separate ways into the smoggy Los Angeles night, neither knowing that this chance meeting would change their lives forever.

"I'm going to marry that girl," Kurt told a friend, who blankly responded, "She didn't want anything to do with you."

Over the next few days, Mary Jo went on with her life, not really thinking too much of the man who smooth-talked her at the bar, but then one day, the rotary hanging on her off-white townhouse wall phone rang.

"Hi, it's Kurt from the bar the other night."

"Oh yeah, hi. How are you?"

She remembered him, obviously, but had to play it cool. Plus, she wasn't sure how she felt about this guy and didn't want to lead him on. Maybe, she thought, she only gave him the time of day because the Chippendales got her feeling eager. One thing Mary Jo knew was that this handsome guy from the bar was not at the top of her priority list.

"You want to go out tomorrow night?"

"I'm busy," she told him.

"How about the next day?"

"I can't."

"Are you available next week?"

"I'll have to check my schedule."

Football players had gotten less painful stiff arms than Kurt was getting. Undeterred, Kurt would not take no for an answer, and the two eventually agreed to meet at a restaurant in La Crescenta, where she lived.

La Crescenta, located about 15 miles north of Los Angeles, was a homey community and the epitome of a place where nothing happens. It's lovely, but La Crescenta's idea of a wild night is a stoplight malfunctioning. That wasn't always the case. Back in November 1933, wildfires scorched La Crescenta's adjacent mountains and seared off all its vegetation. Then, in late December of that same year, an onslaught of rainstorms rumbled through and caused catastrophic flooding. It also soaked the burned and bare mountains, putting them and the town of La Crescenta in a very precarious spot. The worst fears were realized around midnight on New Year's Eve when the trembling mountains saturated from the disastrous downpour couldn't bear the burden anymore and gave way. Mud and debris barreled down the hills like a cascade of dirty lava. It's estimated that over 400 homes were wiped out. Famed songwriter Woody Guthrie even wrote a song about it called "Los Angeles New Year's Flood."

That disaster was all a distant memory when Kurt drove his beat-up pickup up the 110 freeway from Hermosa Beach to La Crescenta in 1983. But the date didn't start as desirably as one would have hoped. It was its own kind of disaster, as the duo missed dinner altogether because Kurt got lost and was two hours late — not exactly the world's greatest second impression. Once he finally got there, Kurt and MJ both subscribed to a heavy liquid diet at a local bar and had deeply resonating conversations.

"What are your parents like?" she asked, only to discover he had no father figure. She asked about his mom and his career.

He asked about her thoughts on children and long-term goals.

Maybe it was the belly full of Coors Light or Kurt's fish-out-of-water outlook on life, but Mary Jo knew she was falling in love with this man, tardiness be damned. She was young, only 21 years old, but she knew this was love. Real love. Call it love at second sight. It struck her that night that she'd be married to Kurt forever.

Oct. 1, 2017: 10:05 pm

"Those are gunshots," CJ immediately pointed out at 10:05 p.m. without hesitation.

Jason Aldean wasn't even halfway into his fourth song of a planned 90-minute set when the enduring sound of faint explosions suddenly infused the night's assonance and emanated more than the singer's voice.

"Are those fireworks?" a confused Mary Jo asked while turning to look at her husband. Kurt, however, wasn't standing there.

When her eyes darted down, she saw her dead husband for the first time on the asphalt. While there's no real way of knowing if he was the first person struck, he was among the first, as Jason Aldean was still on stage singing when Mary Jo saw her husband face down. Instantly, a small red stream started forming as blood flowed out of his warm body onto the blacktop. Rolling him over onto his back, Kurt's eyes were still open, showing his crystal blue irises.

"No Dad, no Dad!" Jessica cried under the Vegas moon as the concert continued.

The gravity of the moment was full-facing.

Hoping she hadn't just seen her father alive for the last time, Jessica threw herself to the ground and speedily began chest compressions.

"Come on, Dad! Come on!"

Push, push, push.

"Come on, Dad! Come on, Dad!"

Push, push, push.

The family didn't want to admit it, but it was futile, and they knew it already. Kurt wasn't speaking, moving or responding to the pounding on his chest through his orange T-shirt that read "In 'Dog Beers' I've Only Had One." Jessica's pace slowed as her father faded to darkness. When she stopped, she lowered herself to give him another hug.

Kurt was struck by a single bullet that hit him in the clavicle and proceeded to travel directly into his heart. His death was abrupt, and he never had time to realize it was happening.

Less than a minute after the first bullets started penetrating the crowd, Mary Jo von Tillow's harsh reality hit her: She would never wake up next to Kurt von Tillow again.

In the midst of this, a deranged gunman was firing upon the whole crowd from his 32nd-floor corner suite at Mandalay Bay, the property across the street from the Las Vegas Village, which acted as a parking lot when it wasn't being used as a concert venue. Tonight, it was a war zone.

February 1983

Kurt was certainly unlike anyone Mary Jo had ever met, and he acted so much older than his age. Having grown up largely fatherless in wine country in Santa Rosa, Kurt and his brother shared man-of-the-house responsibilities for their mother and sister. It wouldn't be fair or factual to say his upbringing aged him, but it certainly made him more worldly than any other 21-year-old Mary Jo ever met. Aren't you supposed to be only consumed with getting laid and getting shitfaced at that age?

"You were really born in the wrong era," she often told him. "You're always talking to old people."

"They have the best stories," he'd respond with a shrug.

No different than men born decades before him, Kurt listened to old-school country music artists like Waylon Jennings and Merle Haggard, two guys who weren't exactly topping the charts in the '80s anymore. Country music at the time wasn't perceived to be cool at all. Kurt's uncoolness was cemented with his sporting choices, too, as he was glued to the TV during NASCAR races, an old man's sport then. He watched golf on television, which was more snoozy than an alarm clock. Ironically, golf and NASCAR both get big ratings on TV now, and country is a hugely popular music genre that continues to grow. It's like Kurt's old soul somehow saw the future.

Mary Jo saw her future, too.

"I think I met the guy I'm going to marry," she told younger sister Jill, with whom she lived at the time.

"You've only been together a few weeks."

"He's different."

"Aren't they all?"

Jill would soon meet Kurt after he came to their townhouse, but the interaction was cut short when Kurt passed out in his future wife's bed after a night of drinking.

"He's such a lightweight," Jill deadpanned, unimpressed.

It was a hell of a first impression for her. Although Mary Jo wanted her sister's approval, which didn't initially come, she didn't really care what Jill thought.

Not long after, Mary Jo upset Jill after telling her she was moving out of their townhouse and moving in with Kurt.

Jill's anger wasn't directed at Kurt or Mary Jo necessarily, but rather at her financial situation: She couldn't afford the townhouse rent by herself and didn't know anyone else she wanted to live with who could also pay their share.

"I can't believe you're doing this to me for this guy," Jill sharply shouted.

"You have every right to be upset at the situation, but don't be mad at Kurt, and don't be mad at me!" As Jill stormed off, Mary Jo bellowed, "We're going to get married!"

Mary Jo was so fully smitten that she easily dismissed Jill's infuriation.

Not wasting time, Kurt and Mary Jo moved to the beach off the Southern California coast and shared their little lover's hut. Jill had to move back home with her parents — a total gut punch. She resented Mary Jo for a very, very long time.

Oct. 1, 2017: 10:07 p.m.

First came the chaos, then came the carnage.

The shower of steel bullets was still raining down on the concert crowd, most of whom were ducking, dodging, fleeing and doing anything they could to avoid getting taken out.

Everyone knew this was bad, but nobody knew how bad things already were. The revelry of the evening was undoubtedly over, and it had been two minutes since Jason Aldean ran off the stage to be with his pregnant wife.

With no good answer as to how to react to the disarray, Mary Jo's group got down on the ground beside Kurt's suddenly deceased body. Only bad options seemed to be at their disposal, but playing dead was the best bad option, as they believed the gunman (or several) were inside the concert venue. As the von Tillows lay there, the house lights of the venue flickered on and off a few times, acting as a warning sign to the crowd, many of whom ran for safety, trying to flee the butchery.

"I'm shot, I'm shot," Kurt's sister Dee Ann suddenly screamed above the gunfire as blood spewed out of her ankle. "I'm shot, too!" her daughter Araina shouted after a bullet traveled through her calf, causing her to hunch over and reach down, her hand clasping her lower extremity.

Sure that her final breath was moments away, Mary Jo couldn't see the bullets zinging through the dark night at 2,700 feet per second; she could feel the slugs peppering the ground and green faux turf around her. Mary Jo could feel the faux grass blades jumping all over her legs as she was being coated by soft shrapnel, fearing the five-centimeter munitions would fatally follow.

Amid her deafening screams, Mary Jo was prepared to die that night. The reality is that with Kurt gone, and he had most certainly taken his final breath, she didn't care if she died with him on Oct. 1, 2017.

The earth beneath the crowd's feet was blanketed with bodies — some people were on the ground for safety, some were shot and some were dead. The live microphones from the stage created an echo for the bullets, which was relentless, only intensifying the fear. And, as if Kurt's lifeless body wasn't enough of a reminder, the family was very exposed with little adequate shelter in sight. Still, at no point did Mary Jo think the shooting was happening from the gold-glistening hotel across the street, nor did that matter much.

Rat-tat-tat-tat, tat-ta-tat.

Rat-tat-tat-tat, tat-ta-tat.

Bullets sprayed at a rate impossible to count, but Mary Jo was not in my right frame of mind, adamantly refusing to leave Kurt and that now-sacred piece of asphalt. Sprawled out on the pavement, lying on her chest, Mary Jo kept her head down as the torrent of tears fell out of her eyelids.

There was nothing to do but wait for her turn to get shot in the back.

Bewilderedly scanning the crowd a few minutes later, she saw pockets of people trying to help others. Random strangers were trying to help her, too. Tiny acts of heroism happened everywhere, including Jessica, who used a bandana and cell phone cord from her purse to create a tourniquet for Araina and her hemorrhaging calf. Still, this was a life-or-death situation, and no one was safe.

"To this day, I can still feel the vibration of the gunfire, and the stench of burning is seared in my mind," Mary Jo says.

Bullets slammed into metal security gates meant to protect and corral fans, and the fragments ricocheted into the masses. Glass windows were being shot out of the three-level VIP suites that resembled refurbished trucking containers on the far east side of the venue, the same area Mary Jo eventually ended up leaving from. Bullets continued to hit the ground and leap up like rocket ships, often finding homes in people's backs, butts and arms. The fear rippling through the 22,000 concert attendees was palpable as the asphalt began transforming from black to a tint of crimson, the result of blood spatter. The panic of that evening was unshakable.

"We have to get out of here," Jessica demanded while watching human beings get mowed down and fall to their death.

For over 10 minutes, almost the entire length of the massacre, the von Tillow troupe lay face down on the ground, but it felt like an hour.

While Mary Jo made peace with dying, a man who turned out to be an off-duty cop ran up to her, sensing something was amiss. "You're going to die," he said as she lay on the asphalt next to her dead husband.

In a disconcerted tone, he added, "You're the only ones that are alive out here."

Mary Jo peeked her head up and saw nothing but doomed fates. It was a country music fan genocide. Still, like how

Kurt was so persistent in getting Mary Jo to go out on a date with him all those years ago, she was equally persistent in not leaving his side, no matter the consequences.

"I'm not leaving him."

"Ma'am, we need to get you out of here."

"No!" Mary Jo demanded.

"Mom, this isn't normal. You're going to get us all killed," Jessica loudly chimed in over the havoc, realizing her mother's stubbornness. She then screamed, "We have kids at home. You cannot do this. You have to get up and move."

Danger be damned, Mary Jo was determined to soak up every waning second with her husband.

1984/1985

Everything happened so fast. Three months after their first date, Kurt popped the question to MJ, and they were engaged. About nine months later, they married. Within a year of tying the knot, they welcomed a son, Matthew, in 1985. Jessica, their second child, came in 1987. Not long after, the newly formed family moved from Southern California to Northern California's Sonoma County and bought a family home for $111,000.

The home, all 1,300 square feet of it, was hardly glamorous but worth every penny. That three-bedroom, two-bathroom abode was their little slice of California — "little" being the keyword regarding the bedrooms, which barely fit full-sized beds. With no primary bathroom, the whole family shared a hallway bathroom, which was hell to keep clean with four people using it. Purchased one week after Jessica was born, the white house with black trim was within walking distance of all the schools.

The kids were perfect characteristic mirrors of their mom and dad; Matthew was more like his mother, tender and pragmatic, whereas Jessica was very much like her dad, stern and ready to throw caution to the wind.

Unlike Kurt's non-existent father, he was active in his children's lives despite working as a trucker, which required him to travel often. Once Matthew and Jessica became teenagers and cell phones were much more prevalent, Kurt would often call them from behind the wheel. The kids remember their dad on the road a lot, driving from border to border and corner to corner, but they also remember him on the sidelines of their games. When Jessica had two children of her own, Grandpa tried as much as possible to be a constant face in their lives.

Kurt and Mary Jo were empty nesters by the time they were in their '40s, as Matthew went off to school at Syracuse University, and Jessica was in college in Denver. Although Kurt and MJ's life was now on easy street thanks to having self-sufficient kids, they knew they also wanted a change and eyed the East.

2005

The next phase of Kurt and Mary Jo's life began in 2005 when the couple packed up and moved from Santa Rosa to a country club in Cameron Park, a small town about 30 miles east of Sacramento and just 20 minutes from Folsom, where Johnny Cash famously performed Folsom Prison Blues for inmates in 1968.

At Cameron Park, things were good. Mary Jo was making a hell of a living as an executive at Bank of America, a company she started working for as a senior in high school and the only company she ever worked for. Her banking career began as a pay file clerk, where she meticulously compared signatures on checks to a signature card to ensure things were valid. In the digital age, that job no longer exists.

Hired by Bank of America on March 6, 1979, she retired on Aug. 31, 2020. Due to her enviable work ethic and company loyalty, she worked her way up the ranks and eventually became a senior executive. At that level of commercial banking, only about 10% were women, as it was a male-dominated division with challenges for young women trying to make their way up the corporate ladder.

"Banking was, is, and will probably always be a man's world," she says matter-of-factly all these years later.

Kurt was doing well financially, as well, and he was hardly frugal. If he had money in his pocket, he wanted to spend it and worry about consequences later — a trait from his mother, who had a "take the trip, buy the shoes, eat the cake" attitude, Mary Jo says. Kurt, she added, adhered to the "live for today, worry about money later" motto.

When Mary Jo met Kurt at that bar in 1983, he was fresh out of school at Wyoming Tech, where he studied to be a diesel mechanic. Kurt was always tinkering with things and was fascinated by tractors, buses and engines, so the job was a natural fit. After graduating, he left the western world of Laramie, Wyoming, for the salt-kissed air of Hermosa Beach and landed a job with Mercedes-Benz at South Bay Autohaus. During those days, the American dollar was especially strong, so well-to-do clientele would buy their cars in Europe, ship them to the U.S. and have Kurt convert them to American standards by ensuring the doors were reinforced and the emissions passed the California smog codes.

After they moved to Santa Rosa, Kurt worked as a mechanic for a few companies but eventually wanted to transition into a driver role. He got his chance when he worked for Andy's Produce in Sebastopol, a farming community adjacent to wine country that seemed to house a significant hippy population, where free love and bare feet were the norm. Dairy farms were once prominent, but vineyards have largely replaced that area. Sebastopol is renowned for its

Pinot Noir and Chardonnay, which thrive in the soil and fog that sweeps over the coastal foothills.

The stint with Andy's opened Kurt's eyes to entrepreneurship, and von Tillow Trucking was born in 1995. Before he died, Kurt built up von Tillow Trucking and owned three trucks and four trailers. He was planning to sell the company to an employee and retire in December 2017.

"I just want to see the grandkids and golf," he said of his post-retirement plans, which were made easier by the fact that his backyard butted up to the 13th green at Cameron Park Country Club.

No hack on the golf course, Kurt had a handicap of about three to six. The average golf handicap for men is around 14.

A golfer since he was five years old, Kurt's great-grandpa, Archie, taught him how to play after cutting down some bamboo shaft clubs. He then paid it forward by teaching the game to his family. For Matthew's 30th birthday, he and Kurt went to Florida to watch the Daytona 500 and play TPC Sawgrass, one of the premier courses in the United States. It hosts The Players Championship every March, and its 17th hole is one of the most recognized in the sport due to the green being surrounded by water. It's called an "island green," even though it's actually a peninsula. That day, Kurt shot an 84, but father and son were just so happy that neither hit it in the water on 17.

Mary Jo wasn't much of a golfer when she met Kurt, but she improved. Kurt, though, was great, and his patience on the links paid off on March 3, 2016, when he notched his first-ever hole-in-one at the 16th hole of Cameron Park Country Club. The celebratory moment is a blessing and a curse because it's a tradition to buy drinks for everyone at the clubhouse when you sink a hole in one. Luckily for their nest egg, this was a random Tuesday in March, and few people were around that day, so Kurt's wallet wasn't damaged too much.

"I got off easy," he laughed. He then drunk-dialed their son to tell him.

Matthew had long been Kurt's outlet of frustration for having exactly zero hole-in-ones on his resume. When he finally got one, his life was made. His golf agony was over.

"I got one! I got one!" he shouted to Matthew, who could hardly understand his dad through the fog of equal parts thrill and hops.

"You got what? What are you talking about?"

"I aced the 16th!"

Matthew's smile could be felt all the way from Ohio, where he lived at the time.

Less than a year later, Kurt scored a second hole-in-one when he aced the 17th hole from 200 yards out during his first senior (over 55) tournament. That, too, was joyous, but there's nothing like the first.

The fact that Kurt was so good at golf wasn't a surprise, given his superb sports skills.

"He was definitely a Sonoma County legend," Matthew said, due to his father's sporting prowess.

Oct. 4, 2017

After Kurt passed in the Las Vegas shooting, the local golf community was "a Godsend," Mary Jo said, noting it donated money so the mourning family could fly private back home, which kept Kurt's ashes undisturbed and not sifted through by TSA agents; it also prevented the von Tillows from openly weeping in front of an unsuspecting Southwest Airlines flight attendant. Mary Jo's sister Jill took it upon herself to coordinate various necessary things in the wake of the shooting, which was right up her alley, considering she has an event planning business.

"You should rename your business to GSD International, for Get Shit Done," Mary Jo told her after realizing all the coordination, which included procuring that private jet.

After Kurt's untimely death, their country club home became somewhat of a pilgrimage for the community, with club members honoring Kurt via a golf cart procession down to the house he and Mary Jo shared. When MJ finally got home after her nightmarish week in Vegas, her backyard was a shrine to the man to whom she had married 33 years prior. In just a few days, a makeshift memorial full of flowers, flags and oversized pictures of Kurt was haphazardly built all over the exterior fence separating the backyard from the golf course. Many friends reflected by sitting against the iron fence, sipping Coors Lights to honor Kurt.

"He was the most friendly and outgoing guy you could ever meet," a neighbor who lived in the country club told the Sacramento Bee. "It's a sad day for the neighborhood. It's a sad day for everyone. This just hit a little close to home."

Less than a week after his death, El Molino High School in Forestville, Calif., where Kurt attended, honored him before a football game, and current players held up their helmets in tribute.

The unassuming school, known at the time for its rust-red roof, abruptly closed for good in 2021 due to declining enrollment and chronic budget problems, but not before producing Imagine Dragons co-founder Ben McKee and Arianne Phillips, a three-time Academy Award nominee for costume design. Kurt, too, was no slouch, as he starred in basketball, football and baseball. As a senior in 1980, he was the starting fullback on the Sonoma County League Champion football team. Donning his number 33, he got his picture on "The Wall" of El Molino's gym, a privilege reserved for only the best student-athletes. A few years before he died, he was inducted into the school Hall of Fame. He didn't even go to the ceremony.

"I just don't have time to go there. I have to work."

Without a hint of ego, he added, "I don't know if I really belong in the hall of fame there anyway."

As revered as he was in high school, Kurt might have been more beloved with age. When Jessica was in college in Denver, Kurt would often drive there, and her friends dropped everything to drink with him... at least until he fell asleep and mimicked *Weekend At Bernie's*. Mind you, as a trucker, Kurt would often wake up at 3 a.m., so he was exhausted by the time he'd made it to Denver.

"We would have the best time and laugh at him, and he'd fall asleep on the bar," Jessica recalls. "He would look awake in the chair but nod off. You'd be sitting at a table with a group of people, and Kurt is just sleeping."

This might have been embarrassing for most college students, but Jessica found her dad's sporadic narcolepsy humorous.

At home, Kurt was just as popular, a local celebrity even, and his distinctive boisterous laugh was equivalent to an invitation into his life. Kurt had quickly made friends with the neighbors when the von Tillows moved to Cameron Park, and their place, all 3,300 square feet of it, quickly became the party house of the community. An unapologetic party guy, Kurt committed to every social event.

Mary Jo, for that matter, was no prude and had fun every time they'd gone out, but sometimes the party grind weighed on her.

"Do we really have to go?" she asked her husband on far too many occasions.

"Yes, I committed to that," he responded on far too many occasions.

Still, they never really fought about their social life. The only real fight the happy couple ever had was about taxes. It was an annual fight. March and April were never a good time in their house.

Mary Jo paid taxes through her Bank of America paycheck. Kurt wasn't a tax cheat but wasn't great about keeping up his books. Mary Jo was furious when noticing he never paid quarterly taxes to the IRS. Although family-owned, von Tillow Trucking wasn't some rinky-dink operation — it was really profitable. You would think Kurt would have a grasp on his finances.

"I hate taxes. I can't golf and see the grandkids because I'm dealing with all this shit," he said.

"Why don't you just hire someone to come in and do this?" his wife forcefully asked once.

Over the course of their three-decade marriage, the couple never had an official discussion on who would handle the finances of their marriage, but it obviously fell to MJ because of her banking background. She always dealt with the family finances, investments and insurance policies. About a year before Kurt's death, it dawned on Mary Jo that her husband wouldn't have any idea what to do if something happened to her, so she created a folder of their assets and put it in an envelope.

"Here's some good information. You should look at it," she said, handing it to Kurt, whose nod suggested he would.

When Kurt died, Mary Jo looked inside her late husband's desk to start clearing it out. There in the top drawer sat that manila envelope, still sealed and unopened. Kurt died not knowing how much money they had, and he was content with that. If he wanted to do something extravagant, he would ask his wife if they could afford it. That was the extent of his knowledge about their assets.

"Kurt knew we had a privileged life, which we worked hard for, but he didn't know if he had $10 or $10 million in the bank," Mary Jo said. The actual number, she jokes, "was somewhere in between."

As is often the case when someone passes in a high-profile fashion, scam artists come out in force looking for a quick payday via false tales. They're circling vultures, waiting to pounce on their prey when they're most vulnerable. Quick to realize this, Mary Jo squashed their hopes.

"We're buying property together and just about to invest. He didn't send us the $30,000 of his portion," one scam artist told Mary Jo on the phone, not realizing that Kurt's financial aptitude was lacking, at best, and started and ended with his wife. It took everything in her not to laugh in that guy's face.

"I'm from Jason Aldean's crew," another person said before Mary Jo hung up. Honestly, no part of her believed the caller was with the celebrated singer's team. That man on the other end of that call was just another grifter attempting to pull one over on a grieving widow.

She was in self-protection mode.

Ironically, if one of those vultures had said Kurt invested in a patriotic company, his wife might have believed it. Kurt's closet was a mounting mass of stars and stripes, and he was often pictured in patriotic shirts. The family all called him Captain America, which he loved. When Kurt was killed, many media organizations showed a picture of him from 2016's Route 91 Harvest Festival, where he donned an American flag shirt. Sunglasses rested atop his faded brown hair.

If only those same news organizations could have seen the last photo Mary Jo and Kurt ever took together, although it might make some newspaper editors shudder.

Before heading over to the festival on Sept. 30, one day before the terrorist act, the family grabbed food at Dick's Last Resort in the Excalibur. A chain, Dick's is a real wildcard of a restaurant, as servers are supposed to be crass, inappropriate and sometimes even rude. That's the schtick, so you'd better have a sense of humor. Guests are encouraged to play along and wear "hats" created from white table paper rolls. The hats all sit tall on guests' heads, almost like a chef's headwear. The custom "hats" always say something silly, controversial or borderline profane, and the staff gets to pen the saying — guests have no control over it, which is part of the fun. In Mary Jo and Kurt's final photo together, she wore a hat that said, "Really?! I shaved my [drawing of a pussycat] for this?" Kurt's hat said, "Broke Back Mtn. changed my life." Brokeback Mountain, which won three Oscars in 2005, was the love story of two male cowboys. MJ couldn't contain her laughter because Kurt was anything but comfortable with that movie.

Oct. 1, 2017: 10:12 p.m.

While Mary Jo was determined to lie by her husband of 33 years, her niece and sister-in-law were whisked away to a triage tent via an unattended, wheeled beer cart some Samaritan found. People who just wanted to help were resourceful and used anything with wheels to transport the injured. Both the off-duty policeman and Jessica eventually convinced Mary Jo to move to an area 20 yards away, where she could still see Kurt but be less in harm's way. Of course, they weren't totally safe, as the shooting was ceaseless, proven by the fact that police investigators ended up recovering 1,057 shell casings from the gunman's hotel suite. What lay in the wake was just utter devastation — bodies just littered on the ground, surrounded by a sea of empty water bottles, smashed beer cans, lost cowboy hats, discarded lawn chairs and blood. So much blood.

"Are you shot?" one person said to Mary Jo over the sound of the gunfire, which was still causing death and ripping flesh and families apart in an instant. She almost had to second-guess if she'd been hit because her clothes were covered in blood from Kurt, Dee Ann, Araina and probably a few strangers, too.

In hindsight, it's hard to believe that she wasn't injured during that 11-minute onslaught, especially when considering half of her group got shot that night. Plus, she'd been standing between Mandalay Bay and her husband.

There was so much mayhem and havoc going on that she temporarily lost sight of Kurt, and Mary Jo was again reverting to her extremely vocal hysteria. As she considered sprinting back to Kurt, someone heard her screams over the gunfire and decided it was a good idea to bring his body over to her. This person, whom Mary Jo didn't know, thought they were doing a good deed by letting the widow of just a few minutes see the lost love of her life. Here's the problem: the dead man brought to Mary Jo wasn't Kurt. It was Jack Beaton, who was also killed that night after being shot in the head.

"Holy fuck!" Jessica uttered upon seeing the fresh corpse of a dead man who was not her father.

"To say this moment haunted me for a long time would be an understatement," Mary Jo admits.

As time passed, she later learned that Jack died while shielding his wife, Laurie, from the gunfire. The couple from Bakersfield, Calif., was celebrating their 23rd anniversary at the festival. After Jack was hit and died, Laurie started leaving the venue, but had second thoughts and turned around. When she returned to the location of Jack's body, he wasn't there. Why was he not here? Where was he? Was she in the right spot? Laurie's heart suddenly filled with hope, thinking maybe Jack was alive. After all, he wasn't on the ground where she last saw him. Perhaps he crawled away, she optimistically prayed. If only. After learning the story, Mary Jo realized she needed to tell Laurie, whom she'd never met, why Jack wasn't where she thought he'd be. It tugged at Mary Jo, but her fellow widow deserved answers to her pressing questions.

Weeks later, Mary Jo got Laurie's phone number. Her fingers trembled as she dialed the number, preparing to tell her fellow widow why Jack's body was moved and where he was moved. It was an emotional conversation, but Laurie could finally put the pieces together and get closure on her unanswered question.

Mary Jo went into total shock and blacked out after the Jack Beaton moment. The fact that she looked a dead man in the eyes who was not her husband stunned her. She was told that CJ and a complete stranger, whom she still doesn't know, carried her out of the venue. Multiple people offered to help, she was later told.

The shooting, mind you, was still not over.

Those 11 minutes felt like an hour.

Fall 2016

A bleeding-heart conservative, Kurt religiously listened to political pundit Rush Limbaugh and was on the far right politically. Ironically, Rush drove Mary Jo crazy, as she was much more of a middle-of-the-road Republican. But Kurt walked the walk, even going to such extremes as refusing to watch movies that featured liberal actors. Naturally, this made it challenging to watch most films since outspoken GOPers Dean Cain, James Woods, Kristy Swanson and Jon Voight aren't in every movie. Kurt was a big sports guy but wouldn't see *Moneyball* because Brad Pitt was in it.

"You want me to watch a movie with Brad Pitt, a liberal? I'm not doing that," he said of the movie based on the story of the Oakland A's team-building philosophy.

"Who cares what political beliefs he has!" his wife replied.

It was a losing battle. They didn't see *Moneyball*.

He even stopped supporting his beloved 49ers after Colin Kaepernick knelt during the National Anthem. Kurt was disgusted at the quarterback for not standing tall during the Star-Spangled Banner. Although Kaepernick insisted his actions were to protest police brutality against Black men and had nothing to do with patriotism, Kurt felt it was un-American.

In 2016, he was thrilled when Donald Trump won the Presidential election. Kurt was (of course) driving his truck to Denver when the decision came in. Despite listening to Fox News on the radio that night, he didn't believe what he was hearing. After all, every news outlet assumed Hillary Clinton was supposed to win easily.

"He's going to win. Trump is going to win," Mary Jo said during a phone call with her husband. "I'm switching between CNN and Fox News, and there's such a difference in body language. Kurt, I'm telling you, Trump is going to win."

Just before the election, Mary Jo and Kurt and a few others were in Ireland on a golf trip and played Trump Doonbeg, one of the then-businessman's many courses. Easily sticking out as Americans, they couldn't go anywhere in Ireland without someone asking about Trump — to many Irish citizens, they only knew him as a reality TV star from *The Apprentice*. When Mary Jo and Kurt went to Doonbeg's clubhouse, she was merely looking for merchandise with just the course name: Doonbeg. Kurt, meanwhile, was looking for anything, literally anything, that said "Trump." Most of the group tried to avoid hats and shirts that blatantly and brazenly said "Trump," but Kurt was actively looking for them.

After he died but before leaving Vegas, the von Tillow family was invited to Nellis Air Force Base because a military Colonel wanted to honor Kurt before heading out on a classified mission. Nellis is one of the largest Air Force Bases in the country and is not far from where they tested atomic bombs in the 1950s. It is sadly apropos that it felt like a bomb hit the von Tillow gang when Kurt died, and they continue to feel the effects every day.

Still in shock from the events of that awful Las Vegas night, the von Tillows were running on fumes when they went to the 14,000-acre military base following the invite from family friend Jay Badger. There, they found out the Colonel wanted to put a flag in the window of his jet in honor of Kurt. The airman actually insisted on flying Kurt's flag personally, and it stayed in the jet's window during the classified flight. The von Tillow family - including Araina, who was also hit by a bullet in the Vegas shooting — watched the jets take off beside the runway. Mary Jo sometimes wonders where the jets went, but the whole thing was so tight-lipped that no one was allowed to take pictures of the planes taking flight that day. That training exercise is still a mystery.

Hours later, the flag that rested in the cockpit and soared in the air above, well, who knows, was given to her after the secret mission finished. Witnessing those jets take off in person would have been a highlight of Kurt's life.

Oct. 1, 2017: 10:20 p.m.

Mary Jo's temporary blackout ended while sitting on the curb outside Gate 5, located on the east side of the festival grounds and across the street from a church. The shooting had stopped. Flanked by her daughter and son-in-law, she was soon shuffled to the Tropicana, where many people were taken for safety. The Trop, a gilded throwback hotel from Vegas's Rat Pack era, was one of the closest hotels to the venue. The building is now nothing but a memory, as its two 23-story towers were imploded on Oct. 8, 2024, to make way for a fancy Major League Stadium. It took just 22 seconds for the buildings to be reduced to rubble. By contrast, the shooting lasted 660 seconds.

On Oct. 1, 2017, there was nothing lavish to behold, as the casino was depressing and decrepit. Water stains, probably from decades ago, blended into the white paint. The Trop, even seven years before its implosion, looked like a dying dog that needed to be put out to pasture. In some ways, the smell of musk floating within the walls was better than the smell of death just a few hundred yards away. As casino floor patrons continued to throw away their money without knowledge of the carnage that took place just down the road, hundreds of festival attendees were taken to an underground ballroom and given white tablecloths to keep warm. Mary Jo's tablecloth was soon beet red and covered in DNA.

"You have to call Matthew. He can't find out from the news," she told Jessica, who started fumbling for her cell phone.

Able to tune out the tension, Jessica looked at her phone silently, gathered herself, thought of what to say and called her brother, who she was certain was snoozing three time zones away.

It was about 2 a.m. when Matthew's phone began vibrating by his bedside. Awakened by the buzzing of an iPhone on a wooden nightstand, he looked at the caller ID but didn't answer, believing he was on the end of a drunk dial of his family screaming a Jason Aldean song into the phone. Jessica tried again and again until he finally picked up. By now, Matthew, who had been to every Route 91 before that year but couldn't get out of a work assignment in Ohio this go-round, sensed something wasn't right.

The phone rang again, and he picked up but didn't answer with a standard greeting.

"Is everything ok?" he groggily asked.

"Matthew," Jessica paused. "Dad's dead."

Certain he'd misheard his younger sister, he asked, "Wait, what? What do you mean he's dead?"

"There was some guy shooting, and we're in the basement of the Tropicana. There's a SWAT team running behind us. Mom is hysterical."

"Are you sure he's dead?"

"Yes, he's in a pool of blood, Matthew! He's dead."

"Are you ok?"

"I'm fine, but Dee Ann and Araina are shot and are already at the hospital. I think they're going to be okay but we don't really know."

Lying atop a queen-sized bed in an Ohio hotel room, his temporary home during a work trip, Matthew was now wide awake but had difficulty processing what he was being told during that chaotic 15-minute chat. Jessica was telling him everything she knew. His mother even attempted to speak to him for a moment, but her hyperventilation prevented him from making out any of the words.

"Stay safe," he said into the phone. "I'm booking a flight right now. I'm coming. I love you."

As the conversation ended, an EMT, there to check on concert evacuees, became concerned when he noticed Mary Jo wrapped in her white tablecloth. Cautiously approaching her, he asked a question, only to be met by a blank stare. While waiting for a lucid response he never got, this EMT looked deeply into Mary Jo's eyes and realized she'd gone into shock.

"We need to get her to a hospital now!" he loudly projected, his voice bouncing off the cavernous lower-level walls of the hotel.

With time of the essence, emergency personnel decided to take Mary Jo to Desert Springs Hospital, a medical center located a stone's throw from the Strip, which police had now shut down as a safety precaution so emergency vehicles could reach the victims quickly. Dee Ann and Araina were already at that hospital.

"Be careful with her," the initial EMT said to another, referring to Mary Jo, as they carefully proceeded to the front door of the hotel. "If she goes into full-on shock, we're going to lose her."

With Vegas on high alert, no one was taking chances, and Mary Jo ended up being escorted out of the Tropicana flanked by a SWAT team. While wearing a blood-stained white tablecloth, she was placed on a gurney and wheeled into an ambulance... and that moment was the opening shot of NBC's *Today* at 6 a.m. on Oct. 2, 2017.

Oct. 2, 2017: Morning

At 7 a.m., the surviving von Tillow flock took a taxi back to Caesars Palace, located in the center of the famed Las Vegas Strip. A dramatic water feature greets guests when they enter the iconic property. Mary Jo and Jessica were still in their dirty, death-dotted clothes from the night before when they stepped through the hotel lobby that Monday morning. Mary Jo's hair was a mixture of day-old hair products and dried, coagulated blood. Her usually fair skin looked like a paint-by-number picture with streaks and patches of dark red plasma — most of it from Kurt, but the blood of others had undoubtedly attached itself to her arms, too. Jessica looked similar. They resembled every character from a horror movie.

"We were in a daze, almost like it wasn't real," Mary Jo said.

Meanwhile, businessmen and businesswomen dressed in fine, pressed suits strolled past them on their way to conventions; a few weary-eyed guests were returning from a long evening at the nightclubs; some early risers were deciding on breakfast; families were joyous and headed out to the pool; a group of tourists waited for an airport shuttle; degenerates attempted to find their lucky slot machine..

"How are these people just living their normal fucking lives?" Jessica, who will tell you she's "hardheaded," solemnly said amid the sound of a man's gleeful shout following a profitable roll of the Craps dice.

After returning to their hotel rooms, the mother-daughter duo spent hours watching as much news coverage as possible on the major networks. They ping-ponged between Fox, NBC, CBS, ABC, CNN, local Vegas news and everything in between. Their thirst for what the hell happened was insatiable. During commercial breaks, they watched videos of the massacre online and read through the flood of text messages. It wasn't schadenfreude. It was more information gathering. Kurt's suitcase, overflowing with clothes he'd never wear again, hovered on a luggage rack beside them.

Mary Jo was glued to the TV, devouring the news, which was more or less shielded from them inside the hospital several hours earlier. It wasn't until that morning — nine hours after the shooting stopped — that they realized the gunfire was coming from Mandalay Bay.

"When your husband is suddenly dead, you don't immediately think about where the bullet came from," Mary Jo says.

Matthew eventually got to town and met his mom and sister at the convention center, where the families of victims were meeting. From his window seat on the Southwest plane, he saw the busted-out golden windows of Mandalay Bay that the shooter had broken and fired through. Tan curtains were blowing out the broken openings into the vulnerable Vegas air. Multiple media outlets published images of those very windows. Matthew, though, didn't want to look, knowing that a man perched in that same spot killed his father.

There was also a significant question remaining: What do we do now? Few people, Mary Jo included, ever had to deal with anything like this. She never got a manual for what-to-do-if-your-husband-dies-in-a-mass-shooting-on-vacation — they don't hand those out at the airport.

At the convention center, surrounded by other families whose loved ones perished the previous evening, Mary Jo was told to file a missing person's report, but she knew Kurt wasn't missing. While consumed with the news coverage, Mary Jo kept seeing aerial views of the concert grounds with bodies all over. Well, she thought they were bodies, but they could have been tarps, sheets or even pools of blood. It horrified her to think that her husband was lying there in the baking sun, but the coroner's office soon assured her that wasn't the case, and the colorful splotches on the ground were not bodies.

Felicia Borla, the medical examiner from the coroner's office, was tantamount to a hero. A slender brunette who has seen no shortage of death since starting her job in 2001, she couldn't have been more caring and sympathetic to the von Tillows' situation. Felicia lives in Las Vegas, went to college in Las Vegas and takes pride in the community. The entire city was mourning along with the victims. The city, too, was hurt and bruised.

"Felicia, can you just tell me when you got him?" MJ somberly asked about 14 hours after the shooting.

"We had a refrigerated trailer that went out here at 5 in the morning and picked him up. He wasn't lying out there all day."

It was a fitting way for Kurt to go. He lived and breathed the trucking industry, so it was meant to be that his afterlife started with a ride in a big rig trailer.

It took a few days before the von Tillows were able to see Kurt's body, days spent crying, talking to family and sitting in silence. In essence, they were all zombies trying to make sense of what had occurred.

"I don't know what or where we ate, but I assume we had food. I probably had to be force-fed," Mary Jo said.

When it finally came time to see Kurt at the morgue, each family member spent a moment alone with him, speaking, praying and holding the cold hand of a man with the warmest heart. The decision was then made to cremate him.

Refusing to leave Vegas without Kurt's ashes, the family took up residence at Caesars until Oct. 7, when they all flew back to Northern California on that private jet, knowing that a funeral service was on the horizon.

Oct. 14, 2017

Raley Field in Sacramento is home to the River Cats, the AAA affiliate baseball team for the San Francisco Giants. It was also the temporary home to the Oakland A's when the team decided to flee the Bay. It's a place where baseball dreams can be realized or fizzle out. Hall of Famer Mike Piazza was once a River Cat. However, the baseball diamond looked much different on Oct. 14, as 1,200 people came to Kurt's services there.

Trying to take as much as she could off Mary Jo's plate, Jill contacted caterers, stadium staff and the mortuary. She did it all. There was a list of things Mary Jo knew she wanted for the funeral: it needed to be outdoors and American flags had to be flying. She insisted that Kurt's company trucks greet guests outside the stadium, and she also wanted a flyover because Captain America, aka Kurt, would have loved it. The problem, though, is that the field is within airport airspace, so that idea was quickly shut down. Even Jill, The Get-Shit-Done queen, couldn't convince the FAA to clear a flyover.

As bad luck would have it, wildfires were ravaging the von Tillows' former hometown of Santa Rosa and much of wine country about 100 miles west of Raley Field. The blazes began on Oct. 8 and incinerated the area for three weeks. Once the flames were finally extinguished in Napa, Lake, Sonoma, Mendocino, Butte and Solano counties, over 245,000 acres were scorched, and it's still one of the costliest wildfires on record. During those three weeks of the inferno, crews came from as far away as Australia and Canada to help put out the flames. On the day of Kurt's service, the buzzing of firefighting airplanes echoed in the stands of the outdoor stadium, the result of planes picking up water in Sacramento before heading west to the blazes. Those planes ended up flying right over Raley.

The von Tillows had their flyover, albeit under inauspicious circumstances.

Kurt's presence at the AAA ballpark wasn't over that day. A few family members returned to Raley almost a year later for Jake Owen's "Life's Whatcha Make It Tour," taking place at baseball stadiums nationwide. Prior to the show, Jessica, Dee Ann and Mary Jo were allowed backstage to meet with Jake and his opening act, Chris Jansen.

"Tell me about him," both artists asked of Mary Jo's lifelong love during the brief meetings.

Both men had a connection to Route 91, as Chris played it in 2016. Jake performed on the main stage in 2017, just before Jason Aldean, and he was still there when the shooting began.

The country superstars listened intently, and Kurt's story must have resonated with them because his picture was again shown at Raley Field 11 months after his death.

"I just met a really neat family tonight, and Kurt had his services here. He was shot and killed in Las Vegas, and I want to dedicate this song to him," Chris said before going into Fix A Drink. And there, during that song, was Kurt's face staring at the crowd on the video boards.

Kurt's face was again shown on screen during Jake's set.

"Mr. von Tillow lost his life that night coming out to a country concert," Jake said from the stage.

At Kurt's services, everyone was given a small card with his picture and a short bio, almost like a makeshift baseball card. Suddenly, there on Sept. 16, 2018, Jake was holding one of those cards, which he read to the sold-out stadium: "Kurt loved his family and his country, the American Armed Services, his friends. He loved golf and beer. He had red, white and blue running through his veins." Jake ad-libbed, "If that ain't country, I don't know what is."

The crowd roared, and Mary Jo lost it. Tears rolled down her face like a faucet had been turned on.

"I'm not sad all the time, but good cries are cathartic," she says.

Oct. 15, 2017, and onward

Imagine getting a condolence card and flowers from almost everybody you've ever known. That's how life was for the grieving Mary Jo after Kurt's services. Her home, now missing its patriarch, had basically transformed into a garden filled with daisies, lilies, tulips, carnations and just about every other flower variety. The scent of all those arrangements and her loneliness was pervasive. After two weeks of tears and condolences, Mary Jo decided to handle her immediate life post-Kurt by being distracted. She never went back to Bank of America after the shooting, as she went on medical leave for PTSD. The leave was supposed to be temporary. She thought she could return after a few months, but was in no shape mentally to return. Although she officially retired in 2020, her last day of work was Sept. 28, 2017. It was a Thursday.

Her life took a drastic turn three days later.

"Busy, I need to be busy," she told herself after the dust had settled and the news cycle moved on to its next tragedy, which was the Santa Rosa fires. That last place she wanted to be was alone inside the home she once shared with Kurt, so she fled and started life as a nomad of sorts.

After losing Kurt, Mary Jo was invited to attend the CMA Awards in Nashville and the Breeders' Cup in Kentucky; she was asked to speak at conventions, including one in Florida for victims of crime.

"This might not be a conventional way of dealing with loss, but this is how I chose to do it," she reflects. "Did I handle the months after Kurt's death well? My mind never questions that. I did what I had to do for me in that moment. I don't judge the way the other 57 families grieved."

"This is exactly what Dad would want you to do," Jessica said amid her mom's laborious traveling. "Keep living your life."

Mary Jo even returned to Vegas a few times. Of course, the city felt different to her (it still does), but she couldn't forget that it, too, was healing and still is. Shortly after the shooting, local residents put together the Healing Garden near downtown, which is about 18 miles south of the Las Vegas Village. The purpose is to honor the 58 victims of Oct. 1, 2017. Surrounded by lush greenery, rundown motels and a handful of pawn shops, including the Gold and Silver Pawn Shop made famous on the History Channel's Pawn Stars, sits the garden. Some might find the location disenchanting and utterly detached from the attack — geographically speaking, it shares no connection with the massacre, but the truth is its erection was organic and built by the city and hundreds of mourning volunteers in just four days. Legend has it that the design was sketched out on a napkin. In public areas of the healing garden, pictures of the 58 hang on weather-resistant wood paneling, and a waterfall with angel wings brings calmness. An oak tree donated by longtime Vegas headliners Siegfried and Roy sits in the middle of a cement heart. Guests are greeted by a quote from Shakespeare's "Romeo and Juliet" etched in a rusted-colored panel.

"When he shall die,
Take him and cut him out in little stars,
And he will make the face of heaven so fine
That all the world will be in love with night
And pay no worship to the garish sun."

Nearly all the families of the 58 contributed something to their loved one's area. For Kurt's, Mary Jo left a pair of boots, pictures, metal signs and a 49ers flag. There's also a Peterbilt license plate and a homemade cross that says "LoveLikeKurt."

The families were all given a plaque with the freedom to inscribe whatever they wanted, and the words are featured at each victim's Healing Garden spot. To honor Kurt, the family wrote of his love for family and country and touted some of his athletic achievements.

"He will be remembered for his love of life, his smile, being kind, his knee-slapping belly laugh, and love of beer," they penned, among other things.

Organizers do a stunningly lovely job of maintaining the Garden, which is open daily but sees a massive influx of people every year on or near the anniversary of the shooting. Tissue boxes and free therapists are typically on-site during surge periods. While none of the Oct. 1 victims are buried there, it's a solemn, special resting place that forever bonds families of the 58 to Vegas.

While settling into her new normal, Mary Jo knew she didn't want to stay in that Cameron Park house. It was way too large for just her. Sure, she loved the area, but residents changed after Kurt's death.

"People, especially men, avoided me because they didn't know what to say or how to act," Mary Jo said. "They feared I'd break down from a simple conversation — or maybe they thought they would. Plus, I always saw that home as our home, mine and Kurt's, and I didn't want to be there without him."

Mary Jo sold the home in April 2018 and bought a townhouse in Cameron Park, a nice landing spot for her, as it was part of the golfing community she'd been accepted into. It never felt like home, and PTSD struggles wouldn't subside. She was having vivid nightmares and wasn't sleeping. Finally, in February 2020, just before the COVID-19 pandemic, she moved to Newport Beach, Calif., where she rests her head in a two-bedroom, one-bathroom condo that's probably a quarter the size of her home in Northern California.

"I don't even own it, but I feel free here."

No doubt now settled into her new life, Mary Jo continues to have people in her corner. Her grief and healing would have been far more difficult without the Cameron Park Country Club community. She's still very close to many friends from there and credits her family with keeping her head above water. Jill's husband, Mark, for instance, watches out for her like a little sister.

Mark and Kurt were incredibly close and bonded over their love of racing and NASCAR. As Mark had no biological brother, he and Kurt had a real brother-type relationship. They agreed on many things but had more than their share of disagreements. Still, like family, they managed to get past their minuscule grievances quickly.

"We would've taken a bullet for each other," Mark said, not intending to be ironic.

Perhaps in a bit of a premonition, Mark and Kurt struck an agreement one day in Lake Tahoe, about five years before Route 91.

"If something happens to one of us, let's make a pact. I will look after Mary Jo, and you will look after Jill," Mark said while sitting on the dock of the deep blue freshwater lake they all visited often.

The sun began setting over the pines surrounding the lake, creating a majestic tone.

"That goes without saying," Kurt replied.

The casually struck agreement wasn't taken lightly. A man of his word, Mark has remembered that pact and is quick to help Mary Jo at a moment's notice. Kurt would have done the same for him if roles were reversed, he maintains. Mourning in his own way, Mark, a local musician, even wrote a song about his late pal in the days after Oct. 1, 2017.

The chorus read: "We should live like Kurt, we should love like Kurt. We should bring the world more laughter. We should eliminate the hurt. If you want to make a difference, sport a patriotic shirt. You should pop a beer and spread some cheer to live and love like Kurt."

It's serendipitous that Jill married Mark, as Mary Jo has known him almost all her life. In fact, the sisters' dad coached Mark's teenage baseball team, and Mary Jo kept the score from the stands. Every time Mark would get a hit, he made a beeline for me to ensure she didn't rule it an error.

"I need to keep my batting average," he now halfheartedly jokes with a dose of seriousness.

Mary Jo accurately and fairly credited his batting average, she assured him years later.

Through all the moves, condolences, nightmares and travels in her new widowed world, Mary Jo didn't truly feel like herself for about four years.

"I was just going through life, not really living it, when it dawned on me that things don't have to be this way," she said. "I could have just laid in bed and had a pity party, but that's not a fulfilling life. That would be wasteful. I have a choice in this matter, too."

After some strong self-reflection, Mary Jo realized she couldn't change what happened on Oct. 1, 2017, but she could certainly change how she went about living.

In Aaron Watson's song "Blue Bonnets In The Spring," he sings of wanting to "pack light and love heavy." That was Kurt to a tee. Mary Jo has tried to cling to that sentiment, too, but there's some guilt.

"I feel like I got the best version of Kurt, and I'm not sure he got the best version of me," she said from the couch of her Southern California apartment as a breeze lightly caressed her face. "We both were incredibly admiring of each other for different reasons, and he probably never felt that I could be better, but I feel that. I wish he could see who I am now. I'm different."

Mary Jo von Tillow, the woman who was seen on the Today show in shock, draped in a blood-soaked sheet, is trying to find some good from her husband's murder. She doesn't want to move on necessarily, but she does want to move forward.

"Maybe there was a reason why this happened in my life. Maybe I can do something for somebody else," she told herself in one of her many moments of inner dialogue.

After meeting so many incredible people directly as a result of Kurt's death, Mary Jo can assure you that good has come from that awful fall evening under the Vegas moon.

She's met a man who won an Atlantic City jackpot and traveled the country performing random acts of kindness to honor his best friend killed, a firefighter killed on 9/11; there's a man who became a lawyer after his sister was slain by the same serial killer who murdered little Adam Walsh; there's a former drug dealer who turned his life around when his father was gunned down in the street in a Dayton, Ohio mass shooting. Mary Jo is the through-line connecting all the individual stories. They've all used tragedy as a transition point.

Although she certainly wishes that Vegas night never happened, the fact is that it did. Meeting all these incredible people — people she would not have interacted with otherwise — hearing their tales of tragedy has created an unlikely patchwork of trauma-linked individuals that endures to this day. These new friendships are her post-Oct. 1, 2017, silver lining.

CHAPTER 2

Tommy Maher

September 2001

Tommy Maher was on 15th Street between 5th and 6th Avenue in New York City, picking up garbage as part of his daily job as a sanitation worker, and it was one of those majestic days in the city where the air was crisp and breathable and the sky was a crystal-clear blue. One day prior, a cold front had swept through the East Coast and drenched the area with rain and thunderstorms, but that storm was all but a distant memory. In some ways, it gave the city a thorough and welcome cleansing. The only thing on people's minds was the Yankees having wrapped up a three-game sweep of the rival Red Sox — giving them a stranglehold on the American League East — and Hurricane Erin, which was spinning about 500 miles east-southeast of the Big Apple. New Yorkers weren't exactly panicking about the Category 3 Hurricane, but were more mindful that it could shift and cause real havoc.

Dressed in his bright yellow vest and battered trash-stained gloves, something he got from 20 years of cleaning up The City That Never Sleeps, Tommy was finishing his route and planned to pick up an anniversary card at a nearby stationary store for his beautiful bride of two years, Cindy—two years had flown by and she was more stunning than ever.

At 8:46 a.m., covered in the city's discarded rubbish, Tommy looked at the sky after hearing a loud, low noise. The thunderous buzz went by him so quickly that he couldn't see the cause of the sound, but it wasn't like anything he'd heard as a lifelong New Yorker, and he was pretty sure he'd heard it all. Seconds later, an earth-shaking bang, almost like dynamite exploding, battered his eardrums. The sea of ground-level parking garages surrounding him seemed to quiver, as did the apartment buildings rising above them.

The date was Sept. 11, 2001.

Tommy, a firefighter with the South Hempstead Volunteer Department since 1984, trusted his gut enough to know that something wasn't right, but he was desperately hoping to be wrong as he walked toward 6th Avenue and briskly headed south. Coming to a clearing among New York's famed skyscrapers, he looked up and could see World Trade Center 1, more commonly known as the North Tower, on fire. He gasped. Thick black smoke was billowing out of six high-level floors of the 1,368-foot building, clouding what was a stunning morning. Judging from the size of the gaping hole about 1,600 feet in the air, it was evident that an airplane plowed into the seminal structure.

Clearly, this was disastrous, but it must have been a terrible accident, Tommy thought. After all, the World Trade Center was unfortunately accustomed to accidents or incidents. In 1975, a three-alarm fire broke out on the 11th floor of the North Tower; in 1993, terrorists detonated a van bomb in the parking garage beneath the North Tower, which ended up killing six people; in 1998, men with ties to the New Jersey Mafia robbed $1.6 million from a Brinks truck as it was unloading money for the Bank of America inside the North Tower. The North Tower, home to the famous Windows on the World restaurant, had been beaten up over the years, but she always dusted herself off.

Tommy, his thick accent prevalent, is a New Yorker through and through — even living in the same Long Island house for over 50 years — so the Twin Towers had always been in his eyeline since birth. The buildings meant something to him and not just because they'd been featured in dozens, maybe hundreds, of TV shows and movies. His father-in-law, Richard, also worked for an insurance company on the 35th floor of 2 World Trade Center, more commonly referred to as the South Tower. This was personal to Tommy in so many ways, but at least his father-in-law was safe. After all, the South Tower was unscathed.

While standing on 6th Avenue, his eye trained on the darkening plume engulfing floors 93 through 99, Tommy's eyes widened in fear as he heard another sickening noise coming from the air and watched a second commercial airliner barrel into the South Tower, which housed 110 stories of offices and businesses.

For nearly an hour, as obsidian-hued soot spilled out of both towers, looking as if the devil himself was continuously exhaling polluted breath.

Then, along with hundreds of stunned people standing outside their cars and cabs in the middle of the street, Tommy was transfixed while witnessing the southern building crumble 56 minutes after that second plane crash. The 110th story fell onto the 109th story, which fell onto the 108th story, and so on.

Inside the South Tower, before the collapse, Tommy's father-in-law had been sitting at his desk, speaking on his work phone, striking a deal. Like everyone in Tower 2, Richard knew of the calamity next door but figured it was an accident, so there was no need to evacuate. That changed at 9:03 a.m. when the second plane hit the South tower, the force of which violently threw him to the ground and disconnected the call.

The North Tower collapsed 29 minutes later, a 38-year-old building that once stood tall now reduced to a pile of rubble, ash, dust and human bodies.

For the next 12 hours, Tommy and his family prayed and hoped Richard was safe, as they had not heard from him. Finally, at about 8 p.m., they got word that he was okay, and he soon arrived home, still covered in dust and ash.

Amidst the worry, Tommy discovered that his childhood friend and fellow firefighter Joe Hunter had responded to the terrorist attack in Lower Manhattan. A television crew even captured footage of Joe entering the South Tower, where Richard worked, to join the evacuation effort. Joe was now missing.

Smarter than most other neighborhood kids, Joe graduated from Hofstra University in 1994, earning a Bachelor of Science in Business Management. However, his passion for firefighting and fire training was his life's calling, first as a volunteer firefighter and later as a professional. As a young Irish kid, he yearned to watch fire engines whizzing through the neighborhood. He lived and breathed the business and was often found studying fire behavior in the firehouse's conference room.

"Everything unfolded, and I never got the anniversary card," Tommy recalled. "My wife understood."

In the 10 days following 9/11, Cindy took care of their 2-month-old daughter, Kelli, at home as Tommy helped with whatever was needed at Ground Zero — he mainly was digging and searching for survivors or removing rubble from the site via a metal bucket. During that painstaking search, Tommy was there to see bodies being removed, and he was there when body parts were found. He was also there when then-President George W. Bush gave his iconic bullhorn speech atop a pile of broken concrete and twisted rebar. There, the Commander-in-Chief thanked those working "The Pile," as firefighters called it, and pledged their work was not in vain.

The President's short, off-the-cuff speech conveyed mourning and standing strong with New York. A rescue worker from "The Pile" famously yelled, "I can't hear you!"

Bush replied, "I can hear you! I can hear you! The rest of the world hears you! And the people - and the people who knocked these buildings down will hear all of us soon!"

Chants of "USA, USA" filled the air. Tommy took it all in, realizing the magnitude and unified patriotism of the moment. Amid the death and rubble, it was a rare moment of happiness and a much-needed pick-me-up.

Since the main pile was smoldering (and would for 100 days), the smell of burnt flesh was as prevalent as the dust, debris, and somberness. Days and months passed, and it was evident that Tommy's childhood pal didn't make it.

Joe's charred and mangled helmet from FDNY's Squad 288 was eventually found several months later, and his family donated it to the 9/11 Memorial & Museum, now located on the footprint of where the Twin Towers once stood. It's the only trace Joe ever found from the wreckage. He was less than three weeks shy of his 32nd birthday on 9/11.

Joe died doing what he loved. Afterward, his firehouse honored him by creating the Joseph Hunter Meeting Room.

"He was all about doing the right thing, about being respectful," Tommy said of his pal. "Don't get me wrong, he wasn't like some priest walking around with a collar on. We've all had our share of some things we shouldn't have done, but overall, he was always about helping people and doing the right thing. He was a real guy, a guy with morals, and I think that's what kind of drew him to the fire service. He was always wanting to help people."

Growing up as teens, Tommy, Joe and other close friends ran around the streets of Long Island together. Everyone knew them, and residents began calling their squad The Hempers, which sounds more like a '50s doo-wop group and not a couple of aspiring firefighters. Prior to Joe's 1996 graduation from the FDNY Fire Academy, he and Tommy were often teammates in the New York State Fire Department Drill Teams, a competition among volunteer firefighters to test their skills against their brethren. Akin to an obstacle course for firefighters, participants measured themselves up by racing cars, testing their ladder skills and using fire hoses. Joe served as the South Hempstead Rascals' hydrant man, meaning he would hop off the truck, get the hose on the hydrant and turn on the water in fractions of a second - at least that was the goal. So serious about the drill, it wasn't past Joe to tell others to go home if they weren't committed.

Like all Americans, particularly New Yorkers, 9/11 is a date seared into their minds. It's the post-Baby Boomer generation's version of John F. Kennedy's assassination. Everyone knows exactly where they were and exactly what they were doing when they heard of the terrorist attacks that day. A meme is constantly floated around social media around the anniversary of 9/11, but it focuses on the day after the attack and speaks of how "unified" the country was. Tommy, though, saw that kindness firsthand from Ground Zero and recalled people from all walks of life handing out water and donating dry clothes to first responders.

"My biggest takeaway from the whole thing was that we need to take care of each other a little better. I know sometimes that could sound corny or whatever, but it just taught me to not have an opinion of anyone or anything and just experience everything," he said. "What happens when we form an opinion is we start to form a judgment. There are some crazy things out there that people do, but if we ask questions first, it makes for a better outcome, in my opinion."

Standing on "The Pile," caused by the worst of mankind, helped Tommy see the best of mankind, and Joe was never far from his thoughts.

With his newfound appreciation for helping out his fellow man or woman, Tommy wanted to do something meaningful. He wanted to honor Joe with his actions. It would take 16 years and the deadliest mass shooting in United States history for Tommy to find a way to honor Joe and help hundreds, if not thousands, of people along the way.

October 2017

He was in the shower washing off a long day's work, but Tommy couldn't stop thinking about Las Vegas and the mass shooting that claimed 58 lives on Oct. 1, 2017. He had no connection to the gambling mecca on the other side of the country, but something about that incident connected with him. For a week, he watched national news cover the shooting, often focusing on the death toll and the shooter. Little was concentrated on the surviving families and the ramifications of this mass casualty event. He couldn't just sit back and do nothing.

As the clean, hot water spewed out of the shower head and rinsed away the daily grind, Tommy thought of Joe, and an idea soon came into his brain. It wasn't exactly unusual for Tommy to have some hasty, heartfelt idea, but most of them were quick deeds, like the time he purchased a brand-new PlayStation video game console for a neighbor's son after the boy's family home had been burglarized. The boy had been inconsolable when he discovered his gaming system was gone in the crime, so Tommy quickly purchased a new one and placed it on the neighbor's front porch. He left no note and never identified himself as the mysterious donor.

Tommy, though, is anything but mysterious. The boy's mother, Maria, and everyone in sparsely populated South Hempstead knew who did it.

"If I had to guess, I'd bet this was your husband," Maria told Cindy one day at the supermarket.

Cindy, ever loyal to her husband, essentially shrugged and smirked. "I don't know what you're talking about."

Still, Vegas was a whole different thing. It's a destination city, a tourist city. He couldn't leave a PlayStation at the home of every victim.

"You're going to think I'm crazy, but I feel like I need to do something," Tommy told Cindy in their bedroom a few days after the attack.

"Okay, like what?"

Sitting on the edge of the bed with the local news playing in the background, Tommy explained his idea, which involved traveling to the hometowns of all 58 victims and doing random acts of kindness. He planned to create little notes to let people know that the random act was done to honor a Vegas victim. Tommy proposed that he would trek to all these cities, not via airplane but rather in his 15-passenger van, nicknamed Bessie, which already had well over 100,000 miles on the odometer.

"You know that this thing was in Vegas, and people from all over the country were there, right?" Cindy said.

"Yes, and I can drive Bessie to all the places. That's the beauty of it."

Cindy, who is used to Tommy's unorthodox ideas, articulated, "I know your heart is in the right place, so I'll support you."

The trip, Tommy estimated, would take 18 days and 9,500 miles to complete. But would Bessie hold up?

A used car purchased in 2014, the Ford E150 Super Duty had been used to shuttle kids around to soccer practices, school functions and volunteer outings for years. Since 2017, it has been used every Thursday to pick up 4,000 pounds of food to deliver to the Pope Francis Food Pantry in Bridgeton, New Jersey. About 250 families picked up meals from the pantry on Saturdays, so less fortunate people undoubtedly depended on Tommy and his van. Always seeing the van as more than just a mode of transportation, he used oversized stickers to spell out "PAY IT FORWARD" on the driver's side after purchasing it. On the rear of the van, he included a quote from John F. Kennedy that read: "One person can make a difference, and everyone should try."

The van is an extension of The Honor Network, the non-profit organization Tommy started after the Oct. 1, 2017, shooting in Las Vegas. It always has a Bible in the glove box and a picture of Joe Hunter on the dashboard.

1997

Cindy Pinnavaia was packing her suitcase from her home in Delray Beach, Florida, getting ready to head north to New York for her brother's wedding. She was thrilled for her sibling, yes, but she was excited about this guy from Long Island whom she'd been speaking to on the phone for weeks. They'd never met before, but two mutual friends brought their voices together, and a connection developed quickly.

Relatively new to her job with a credit card company called MBNA, Cindy didn't exactly plan on moving from South Florida, nor was she trying to think past the blind date. She was, however, already feeling loved up and curious to put a face with the name. Tommy, on the other hand, knew what he was getting himself into, as he cajoled the mutual friends to show him a photo of Cindy.

When Tommy walked into Cindy's life that day, she knew in her heart that she was looking at her husband. It was love at first sight.

"I'm going to marry him," she would tell a friend a week later.

Wanting to be closer, Cindy transferred to a similar job in Maryland, and soon after, she moved to New York. Not wasting time, Tommy popped the question a few months after Cindy became a Big Apple resident.

Two years after that blind date, Tommy and Cindy tied the knot outside at a stunning Long Island estate before 175 casually dressed guests on a picture-perfect September 11, 1999. The estate looked out over Moriches Bay and was exquisite and iconic. Called The Lindenmere, it dates back to the early 1900s. Originally built as a residence, it was later converted into a hotel and a bed and breakfast with 14 rooms. In 1981, the estate was purchased by Filipino President Ferdinand Marcos and his shoe-loving wife, Imelda Marcos. History be damned, Cindy felt no pressure regarding her wedding footwear — she wore Converse, which would probably make Imelda Marcos gasp in horror. None of that mattered, given that the Marcos family no longer owned The Lindenmere on Tommy and Cindy's wedding day.

Two kids, Kelli and Ryan, followed.

November 2017

With $1,000 in hand and flanked by Kelli and her friend Aline, Tommy hit the road in Bessie on Nov. 7, 2017. It was election day, albeit mainly for local races. After nearly six hours on the road and a few Big Gulps later, Bessie pulled into Shippensburg, Pennsylvania, a small borough in the southern part of the commonwealth about 25 miles from Gettysburg. Shippensburg was the hometown of Bill Wolfe Jr.

Bill, a Little League and youth wrestling coach with two teenage sons, attended the Route 91 concert with his wife, Robyn, as part of their 20th wedding anniversary weekend. They were high school sweethearts. According to family members, Robyn refused to leave Bill's side after he was shot, her brother went on to tell media outlets. But, as the bullets continued to rain down, she made the difficult decision to leave her husband to save herself. The following day, the coroner confirmed that Bill was deceased. His body was found near the front of the concert stage. Robyn would later say that her life "disintegrated" that evening. A GoFundMe was set up for the Wolfe family, and it raised over $81,000.

Five weeks after that evening, Tommy was parked the van on the main drag of Shippensburg and didn't know what to do. It was 11 a.m., and the place was a ghost town. This trip, which looked good on paper, was just a few hours old and already not going according to plan.

It was then that Tommy spotted Towne Cleaners, a dual dry cleaner and laundromat, and he concocted an idea: he would help pay for everyone's laundry. Shippensburg is a town of about 5,500 with just one high school, so citizens' lives are often intertwined. When Tommy approached the owner of Towne Cleaners to explain his idea, he discovered that the owner and Bill were incredibly close. The man was mourning and had been helping out Bill's widow and her sons.

"Do whatever you want," the emotional owner told Tommy, who now viewed his idea as confirmation that this trip was valid and virtuous.

Before leaving money for people at the laundromat, Tommy wrote a bunch of notes and stuffed them into envelopes. "Please accept this random act of kindness in honor of Bill Wolf Jr." He then left the money and notes on top of the washing machines. Without fanfare, it was off to the next city, and the one after that, and the one after that. Eventually, he called it an "Honor Trip," as he was honoring victims.

As he got deeper into the trip, Tommy delved into the 58 Route 91 victims' lives to make sure his random acts of kindness honored their interests — if a victim were into basketball, per se, Tommy would leave five or six new basketballs on a neighborhood court; if a victim were passionate about coffee, Tommy would go to a cafe and pay for everyone's java; a pet lover might be honored with Tommy handing out bags of dog treats or gift cards to PetSmart. As always, a note would accompany everything so recipients would know that the good deed was done in the name of a Route 91 victim. For Neysa Tonks, who left behind three sons on Oct. 1, 2017, Tommy attached $40 to someone's bike in Arizona. The rider needed some "uplifting," Tommy said. Neysa wasn't a biker, nor was she from Arizona, but it was her birthday, so Tommy's kind acts were all done in her name on July 27. He's left brand new toys at playgrounds, backpacks outside schools, fishing equipment by a local wharf, gift cards outside of fast-food restaurants and even a winning $50 lottery ticket at a convenience store — all of which he never wanted notoriety for.

More often than not, he went to a city with no plan whatsoever, but things always seemed to work out. Over time, he developed a motto: "Trust the process." (The Philadelphia 76ers popularized the same phrase from 2013-2016 in hopes of drafting a team worthy of an NBA championship. Tommy was more successful.)

Once Bessie had rolled into Reno, Nevada, during that initial trip, Tommy's daughter and her friend had to head back to school, so they boarded a plane back to New York. Cindy, though, wasn't about to let Tommy do this alone.

On Nov. 18, 2017, Cindy joined Tommy in Reno, where Route 91 victim Austin Meyer lived. Austin had recently enrolled in Truckee Meadows Community College's transportation technologies program. While celebrating his 24th birthday with his girlfriend at the Las Vegas music festival, Austin was shot and later pronounced dead at University Medical Center, the same hospital in which Tupac Shakur took his last breath.

After honoring Austin in "The Biggest Little City in the World," Tommy and Cindy were set to depart when they came across a woman named Jennifer, who was spotted pushing a shopping cart full of clothes through the center of town. Her young daughter, Hailey Robin, stood by her side. Donning a dark jacket, deep pink lips and windblown hair, Jennifer had just spent her entire paycheck on a pet deposit for their new apartment, but she didn't have money for food, supplies or Christmas gifts for her children. Down on her luck and too proud to ask for assistance, she filled up a shopping cart of possessions and planned to sell them in various Reno parking lots.

"What do you need from us," Cindy asked Jennifer and her daughter, who was clinging to mom like Saran Wrap.

"If we could just get money for a bus ticket, that would be a lifesaver."

Tommy and Cindy did Jennifer one better, handing her $350 in honor of Austin.

As he hopped back into the ripped cloth driver's seat of the van, Tommy felt he was doing something meaningful and decided he didn't want to stop doing random acts of kindness and determined that he would continue touring the country following other mass casualty events.

First, though, he knew the next city on his docket would likely be the hardest.

November 21, 2017

When Tommy finally drove ole Bessie to Vegas, he came upon a city resembling a boxer in the final rounds of a fight, trying his best not to be defeated. A pall was in the air and the Las Vegas Village was still roped off. It was still considered a crime scene. Marquees of restaurants, shops, billboards and some of the world's most famous casinos flashed the words "Vegas Strong." A benefit concert featuring Imagine Dragons, The Killers and Wayne Newton was scheduled to raise money for victims. Blood banks were still getting volunteers. There were constant reminders of Oct. 1 all over the city. The shooting was all anyone was speaking about for weeks.

The Vegas area, home to about 2.33 million residents, felt like it was on a knife's edge. The only thing giving residents hope was the winning streak of their expansion hockey team, the Vegas Golden Knights, who would, against all odds, make it all the way to the Stanley Cup Final before being bested by the Washington Capitals.

Vegas was also different for Tommy's purposes. At all the stops along the way, Tommy was honoring a person. In

Vegas, it was as if he was honoring an entire town, a broken town that felt like it had busted at the blackjack table. Tommy visited a few hotels and faith-based organizations. He spoke about his journey at Destiny Church, and the pastor spoke of the "ripple effect" Tommy's good deeds could have. After befriending that pastor, Tommy found his way to a prayer tent near the Oct. 1 site.

"Tommy, I want you to meet Karla," pastor Bobby Tyler motioned, centering his attention on a petite brunette woman with a thick Southern accent.

Karla — who everyone knows simply as "Karla with a K" — had no connection to Las Vegas before Oct. 1. Living her whole life in Alabama, she'd never been to Vegas before. But, similar to Tommy, she felt a calling to be there, as she was still dealing with trauma in her own life. First, she'd been in an abusive marriage. Following a divorce, she was stalked by a man at her church who would eventually break into her home and hold her hostage for 12 hours. During that ordeal, she was beaten, starved and humiliated. Fearing for her life, she lost her innocence, much like everyone who attended the Route 91 Harvest Festival.

"He didn't kill me, but he killed everything about me," she said of her stalker. "I died. It was just that my body was above ground, and I was still breathing."

Tommy and Karla hit it off, and he spoke of his plans to continue honoring victims of tragedies. As she applauded his decency, he floated the idea of letting her tag along. While intrigued, she wasn't sure this line of charitable work was for her. She even tried to back out of the first trip she agreed to go on.

"Karla, you're going," Tommy simply told her.

"I just don't know if I can do this."

"Karla, you can't see it now, but this is going to be your life's work," he said, mimicking his inner Knute Rockne. "People need someone like you to comfort them in times of need. They need someone to care about them, to listen to them. This thing doesn't work without you."

Karla has been riding shotgun in Bessie since that day. Shotgun. Not driver.

"He only lets me drive when he is hallucinating from lack of sleep," Karla says, noting that she's only driven Bessie twice in six years. And she got the same stern speech both times from Tommy.

"Two hands on the wheel. It's loose steering. Don't go over the speed limit. Don't text and drive."

Karla credits Tommy with helping her get past her own demons. "I tell Tommy all the time I would never have gotten to the place where I am and healed without him."

When Tommy and Karla first set out on their adventures, each trip had a name tied to the number of deaths associated with a tragedy. Honor 58 was the Vegas trip; Honor 9 was their Dayton, Ohio trip; Honor 23 was the name of the El Paso, Texas, trip. Unfortunately, the numbers started repeating, so Tommy simply dubbed his operation The Honor Network and officially formed a 501c(3) non-profit organization.

The Honor Network had a presence at Parkland, Florida, where a troubled teen shot and killed 17 teachers and students at Marjory Stoneman Douglas High School. Tommy and Karla went to Pittsburgh after an antisemitic terrorist attack at the Tree of Life Synagogue. They went to Santa Fe, Texas, after a school shooting where 10 people perished. Of course, they were doing random acts of kindness all along the way to pay tribute to the victims. In Texas, they left gift cards around a GameStop to honor Jared Black, an avid gamer. In Utah, the well-traveled duo stumbled upon a man whose tire had come off his car. Tommy fixed the tire in the name of USMC SSG Taylor Hoover, one of 13 Americans killed in a suicide bombing in Kabul, Afghanistan. On a Michigan roadway, just days after three students were killed during a shooting at Michigan State University, another tire fix hit home.

"You're from New York?" the man dressed nicely in a suit asked after seeing Bessie's license plates. "What brings you out here?"

He made small talk as Tommy installed the spare tire on the SUV. The men couldn't be farther apart based on appearance: Tommy was clad in a wrinkled t-shirt and jeans, whereas the kind-faced man was in his Sunday best. A pocket square peeked out of his jacket.

Tommy explained that he was headed to East Lansing to honor the three victims killed on Feb. 12, 2023. As the man heard the explanation, something changed in his demeanor and his eyes welled up with tears.

"My son goes to MSU and lives right across the street from where the shooting happened."

Tommy, not a talker but usually never at a loss for words, didn't know what to say. He, too, was overcome with emotion. There, on the side of a busy road an hour outside of East Lansing, the teary-eyed man hugged Tommy so tight that they could feel each other's heart beating.

"Take this," the man said, handing Tommy $300 to go toward The Honor Network, "you've restored my faith in humanity."

Together, Tommy and Karla have probably crisscrossed the country 10 times and met hundreds of victims' families. They often hand out metal signs or coins on their trips that read: "Believe There Is Good In The World." The "Be The Good" parts of the sign are always highlighted in different colors or fonts to make those particular words stand out.

Nearly all of The Honor Network's random acts of kindness are chronicled on Facebook. Prior to the Vegas shooting that took Kurt von Tillow's life, Mary Jo von Tillow wasn't on Facebook. In the months after the shooting, she joined as a way of keeping in contact with the families of the 58 victims. She had no plans to be on social media to communicate with others, certainly not some guy from New York she'd never heard of.

"Who's Tommy Maher, and why is he going around doing acts of kindness and using Kurt's picture?" her cousin asked one day over the phone.

"Tommy Maher? He's using Kurt's picture? I've never heard of him. What's his deal?"

After so many con artists tried preying upon her in the days after her husband's death, Mary Jo was suspicious of everyone and wondered if this Tommy Maher guy was making money on Kurt's name. Was this a religious thing? A political thing? After deep diving into his Facebook, she felt he seemed noble and couldn't find anything dubious about him. She assumed he was rich or had a trust fund, as these random acts of kindness for people he never knew couldn't be cheap.

April 2018

Mary Jo was on the East Coast to see her daughter, Jessica, and her two kids, when she connected with Tommy via Facebook and met him at a restaurant in Bryant Park in New York City. She was nervous, glancing at the clock on her phone as she waited. When Tommy walked in, she recognized him immediately from social media. He gave her a warm smile while officially introducing himself, and Mary Jo almost instantaneously felt at ease.

"All my anxiety disappeared as we sat for lunch and spoke about his intentions. Within 10 minutes, I knew Tommy was legitimate."

Donning a light blue t-shirt, sneakers and not even the faintest hint of self-righteousness, Tommy opened up about the reason he decided to travel the country to pay homage to people he'd never met. His "why."

"My buddy Joe died on 9/11, and I just couldn't believe how kind people were after that. Ever since then, I just felt compelled to do something. I promised myself I would do something," he said while sipping an iced tea.

Mary Jo discovered that he helped the recovery efforts in the aftermath of Hurricane Sandy, which smashed into New Jersey and New York (especially Long Island) in 2012. There, Tommy drove his van daily to Restaurant Depot to pick up rice, pasta, fish and anything else to feed his fellow Long Islanders. He took Bessie to Texas and Louisiana two months prior to Vegas to help with the efforts after Hurricane Harvey destroyed the area, as well. Before Vegas, most of his kindness stemmed from weather-related instances.

Tommy seemingly felt comfortable with Mary Jo and asked if she wanted to go on an Honor trip with him. She was hesitant but agreed to meet him in Thousand Oaks, Calif., following the Nov. 7, 2018, shooting at the Borderline Bar and Grill, which claimed the lives of 12 innocent people. She later joined Tommy in 2019 in Dayton, Ohio, and Virginia Beach, Virginia, after more senseless violence.

Those trips and doing random acts of kindness on behalf of the victims "all helped me in my healing process," Mary Jo said.

During the stop in The Buckeye State, she met a soon-to-be lifelong friend. Dion Green had been picking up the pieces of his life after a series of tornadoes struck Dayton. A few weeks later, Dion, flanked by several family members, including his father, Derrick Fudge, headed to the city's Oregon District for a night of revelry. The area is known for its restaurants, coffee shops, bars and nightlife, but this particular evening was anything but revelrous after a masked gunman opened fire around 1 a.m. on Fifth Street.

A barrage of senseless gunfire followed as Derrick, Dion and his fiancée lay on the sidewalk outside a pub.

Although the shooting didn't last long — police were able to kill the suspect within 32 seconds — it had lasting impacts. Nine people were murdered and dozens of others were injured that night. Dion's father, Derrick Fudge, was among those killed after he shielded Dion from the bullet spray. Derrick Fudge died in Dion's arms as his son begged him to "get up."

It was the deadliest mass shooting in Ohio in 44 years.

Mary Jo was more than a little averse to meeting Dion just six weeks after the horror in Dayton, assuming they had nothing in common other than a loved one dying in a mass shooting. Dion was black. She was white. Dion, in his mid-30s, was a case manager at a homeless shelter. Mary Jo was in her late 50s and retired. He was engaged. She was a widow. He was from the Midwest. She was a California girl. He was liberal. She was conservative.

"Just stay for a little bit," Tommy urged after hearing her reservations. "If you're not comfortable at any point, you can just say you're going to the bathroom. Just leave and not make a big scene."

That type of exit, leaving without anyone knowing, is called the "Irish goodbye," which Mary Jo is classically trained in. In fact, she prefers it. Her husband was never an "Irish goodbye" kind of person, wanting to ensure he spoke to everyone before exiting a situation. Opposites attract.

At an Irish pub, fitting for the likely Irish goodbye, Mary Jo wasn't sure what to expect of Dion, but whatever it was, he shattered those expectations. While sitting at a table full of bangers and mash, shepherd's pie and glasses sweating with condensation, Mary Jo and Dion swapped stories and realized how similar their circumstances were. Dion was feeling a lot of guilt because his father was only in Dayton for him. He was rightfully raw and angry, and his relationship with his fiancée was on the verge of collapse. Like Kurt's situation, people came out of the woodwork claiming to be related and seeking money. The California woman who was certain she'd have no connection with Dion felt a kinship. She'd been there, done that.

Without blinking, she gave Dion her number and told him to contact her for any reason and at any time.

Over the years, that contact came in the form of phone calls and an annual Christmas card.

She says, "Who knew that I'd gain a friend that day."

Trust the process.

While Mary Jo clocked out of the banking world and Tommy is retired from New York City sanitation, Karla works full-time as a manager for Walmart in Cullman, Alabama, a city located about 50 miles between the better-known areas of Birmingham and Huntsville. She maximizes her days off and uses all her vacation days for the Honor trips, saying it's "something that I can't not do — I know that's a double negative."

Cindy calls Karla a "godsend." (She also calls her "Luke Bryan" because of Karla's pronounced southern accent.)

Although Tommy and Karla are very much the pilots of The Honor Network, Cindy is more of the air traffic controller doing the behind-the-scenes work, whether that be arranging the hotel rooms on the road, planning their routes or handling the finances, which obviously stack up.

Following the early days of Tommy's Honor trips, Tommy and Cindy's savings accounts were depleted, and their credit cards had racked up about $40,000 in debt. The donations were minimal, and expenses were piling up. There were lean, lean years.

Cindy understands why people weren't lining up to help the cause.

"Are you really going to donate to some stranger that you've just met for the first time hearing this kooky story? I mean, the whole thing sounds completely out there," Cindy says. "In the beginning, it was hard. No one was donating. If they did, it was small. We just had to trust the process, which is what Tommy always says."

The Mahers even rolled their debt into the mortgage, allowing them to keep up with their mounting credit card bills. Over time, though, people began understanding what Tommy was doing and donations came in. Mary Jo even made a $27,000 donation to The Honor Network. A woman from a Long Island bank once organized a fundraiser that poured $11,000 into Tommy's passion project.

"The financial part has changed," Cindy says. "We aren't swimming in the tens of thousands, but we have enough to make sure that he can do what he needs to do for each trip."

May 2023

It had been a while since Tommy and Karla had been out on an Honor trip (thankfully, in many ways), and donations had somewhat dried up. With little on his plate, Tommy joined a group of firefighters for a weekend in Atlantic City's Borgata Hotel. It was Cindy's birthday weekend, but she was completely fine with him opting out of cake for some good-natured debauchery with his pals.

Before heading to "Monopoly City," Tommy did something he'd never done before heading to the casino: he prayed.

"God, let me win some money so I can continue to do what I do," he said to the heavens.

It didn't feel wrong to pray for money, but it didn't feel right, either.

With a view of the marina in Renaissance Pointe, Borgata is arguably the nicest hotel in the area. It boasts

17 restaurants, a 3,200-square-foot Roman-style outdoor pool, a luxurious spa and reflective gold glass that can be seen for miles. It's the top-grossing casino in Atlantic City. When Tommy was there in May, he wasn't concerned with the amenities. This was about spending quality time with his firefighting brothers. The evening at the casino started with a few cocktails and some gambling — the clanging and music of the slot machines became a bit like white noise in time. It was getting late, and all Tommy wanted to do was smoke a cigar with a friend before calling it a night. Knowing cigars were allowed in the high-limit room, he strolled past the craps and blackjack tables and headed straight for the cream-colored arched entryway of Miralto, the Borgata's high-limit slot lounge, which featured over 100 machines.

Adjacent to the hotel lobby, Miralto had recently been renovated and reeked of beauty. Mid-back chairs were adorned with blue and white cow patterns and bright chandeliers lit up the area more than Tommy's cigar. Artificial greenery beautifully broke up the monotony of the light color patterns.

It was about 11 p.m. when Tommy strolled into Miralto, plopped down his rear end on a twisting stool in front of a Wheel of Fortune slot machine and let out a sigh like an old man that could have been either painful or pleasant.

"Ahhhhh."

Getting comfortable and trying not to calculate his casino spending, Tommy lit the match to fire up his stogie, which touted itself as being hand-rolled in the Dominican Republic.

Holding the cigar between his pointer and middle fingers, he wrapped his lips around the tobacco leaves, took in a drag, swirled the smoke in his mouth and blew it out.

"I'm going to put $100 in and see what happens," he said nonchalantly to a friend, a fellow tobacco enjoyer.

In high-limit rooms, $100 won't get you far, but guests can get a couple of spins.

Tommy's first spin amounted to nothing. That was a waste of money. His second spin offered similar results. Nothing.

He took another drag from the cigar. Again, he swirled the smoke in his mouth, tilted his head back and blew out the gray smoke up until the circulating casino air. Thankfully, the casino had a great air filtration system.

On his third spin, Tommy looked at his cigar to see how much was left and wasn't paying much attention to the three reels rapidly spinning. First, a pink 7 showed up, followed by a second pink 7. Finally, a third pink 7 locked in place. The machine screamed. Still, Tommy didn't know what had happened and couldn't see the winnings. Desperately searching for his eyeglasses, he fumbled around in his pocket before grabbing hold of the spectacles and putting them on.

He excitedly looked hard at the howling machine. His pupils grew.

"I won $2,900!" he shouted amid high-fives from everyone there.

Through the plume of cigar smoke, an unknown man standing behind Tommy quizzingly studied the machine. His eyes darted from the reels to the payout chart above them. He looked again. Then, a third time.

"You didn't win $2,900," he told Tommy, his voice cracking from excitement.

The man was right, but his follow-up statement came too fast for Tommy to even consider being disappointed.

"You won $2.9 million."

"What?"

"You hit the jackpot!"

"Holy shit! Is that what pink 7's mean?"

As expected, Tommy went through the roof, enthusiastically screaming. He prayed for money, but he never expected this. Certainly not this much money!

At 11:30 p.m. that night, birthday girl Cindy was sound asleep when her phone rang. She rolled over and noticed Tommy's name flashing across the screen.

"Hello," she said in an anxious and annoyed tone, wondering why in the hell her husband was calling her at that hour.

"You're not going to believe this, but I just hit a jackpot. $2.9 million."

"Tommy, you don't know what you're looking at. How drunk are you? You don't know what you're talking about."

He was so animated that he wasn't making sense, almost speaking gibberish. Cindy, in fairness, wasn't trying to pour cold water on the moment, but she didn't believe for a moment that her husband had won nearly $3 million. Still, he persisted that he had won big.

With the soundtrack of a busy casino in the background, Cindy told Tommy to FaceTime her so she could see his alleged win, almost certain that he was pranking her or just plain wrong about this supposed jackpot.

He did just that, and via a 6-inch iPhone screen, America's newest millionaire showed his wife the machine and the payout. Within seconds of the call, multiple men in suits surrounded him, all of whom were verifying the win and protecting Tommy.

"$2.9 million!" he said, repeating, "$2.9 million."

Cindy squinted her eyes to read the machine via the iPhone before they widened as reality set in. Instinctively, her hand reached upward toward her mouth to cover it, and she began crying. Holy shit, her husband really did just hit the jackpot!

"I gotta go," Tommy told her. "I have to fill out a bunch of paperwork for the IRS."

"I love you."

This was turning into the best birthday trip ever for Cindy, and she wasn't even there!

Although it was pitch black outside and a few minutes past midnight, Tommy's wife was now wide awake, and her heart was racing. Seeing her reflection in the microwave door windows, she looked like she'd been crying, which she had (happy tears).

Still gathering herself amid the unexpected wake-up call, her phone received a text from her husband, a picture of the machine and the payout, which she saved the image for posterity.

Feeling antsy and wanting to scream for joy, Cindy lost her bearings and wasn't even sure of the time on the clock when she dialed Karla's number, but she knew her 'Bama buddy would be awake at Walmart, where she worked the overnight shift.

On the second ring, Karla picked up. It was 12:30 a.m.

"What's wrong?"

"Luke Bryan," Cindy said, using her pet name for Karla. "I'm going to send you a picture, and I want you to look at it and tell me what you think."

Confused and slightly worried, Karla stayed on the line until her phone dinged and opened up the conversation thread with Cindy. She then touched the minuscule image she'd just received to enlarge it. The photo was of a winning slot machine.

As Karla studied this image of a slot machine, Cindy announced, "Tommy hit that."

"You're lying."

The women shared a joyful squeal before Karla started sobbing.

"I'm crying bitch, baby tears, Cindy," she declared. "No one deserves this more than you two."

A few weeks later, Karla flew from Alabama to New York to hug the new millionaires.

People like to romance about winning big sums of money. When the Powerball or Mega Millions lotteries get up to unimaginable numbers, news crews love to ask people what they would do if they won. The answers are usually the same, as people typically proclaim they want to retire and travel. For Tommy and Cindy, they've done none of that. She still works, and he's still the fire commissioner in South Hempstead, an elected position. They still live in the same house (the same one Tommy has lived in for 50 years) and haven't made any extravagant purchases. In fact, they haven't even touched the jackpot that came from the one-armed bandit, choosing instead to invest it so their kids can have a better life. In his exact words, Tommy wants to "change the wealth status" of his and Cindy's children by letting the money grow.

Trust the process.

Oct. 6, 2023

Tommy Maher rises at the ungodly hour of 3:30 a.m. every day like clockwork. He readies himself and gives life to his house by opening three shades. Out of habit, he always glances to the corner of his block to see Bessie. He then walks out the door and is at the gym lifting weights, riding a bike or running on a treadmill by 3:55 a.m. His routine is very stringent, and, like the post office, neither snow nor rain nor heat nor gloom of night, or morning in this case, will stop him.

This day started no differently, that is, until he noticed something, or rather a lack of something, on the street. His van, the one that carried him all over the country to do random acts of kindness for fallen people, was gone. Never one to break his routine, he somberly went to the gym. In his mind, he knew the van was stolen, so what was he going to do? Besides, people have things stolen from them every day, he thought.

Following the workout with his mind preoccupied, Tommy came home, called the police and filed a report. He was nonchalant about Bessie's absence. In contrast, Cindy was dumbfounded as she sat with her hands on the kitchen table.

"Are you sure someone didn't take it to do some good with it?" Cindy asked her husband, as a picture of his jackpot sits over her shoulder.

"I'm sure."

"Who would want a van with 'Pay It Forward' on the side?"

At the time of its theft, Bessie had 255,000 miles on her. It's because of her that Tommy's Honor Network is even possible. That van, for all her flaws, carried so many memories. Granted, it broke down too many times on Honor trips and even had the catalytic converter stolen once in California. Often, repair shops would waive the price after finding out what the van was being used for. When you put "Pay It Forward" on the side of a vehicle in giant letters, it tends to spark up a conversation! A friend even resurfaced the cloth seats for free because of a foul smell emanating from them.

"Does it have a security system?" the insurance agent asked Cindy when she called to report the theft.

"A security system?" she replied, laughing at what she thought was the best joke she'd ever heard. "It's a 2001 van. We're lucky it had automatic windows. It still has a cassette player in it."

Coincidentally, not long before the van fell under new ownership, Cindy had broached the topic of getting a new van. She'd been increasingly worried about him breaking down on the road... again. There was even idle talk of replacing Bessie after Tommy's Atlantic City win.

"I'm not ready," he said. "I think she's still good."

He always put Bessie up on a pedestal, thinking of the van as a bit of a family member.

For as emotionless as Tommy was about the theft, Karla was the exact opposite.

"We have witnessed so many things in that van, and we've stopped and helped so many people in that van. We've had long talks where I've been able to lean on him, or he's been able to talk about 9/11 and lean on me. We've picked up homeless people; we've fed dozens of people; we've picked up people whose cars were broken down. It's just so special."

Because of Bessie's deep links to Tommy's random acts of kindness, he felt the need to let everyone know his beloved van's fate.

"My heart is heavy and hopeful, at the same time, as I have learned over and over to trust the process. My van was stolen last night from right in front of my house- my PAY IT FORWARD van is gone," Tommy penned to his social media following.

"As I have only had a little while to let this sink in, my thoughts go to how many people Bessie helped in my hometown. Bessie has been part of my dream that became reality. When 9/11 happened, Cindy & I knew we wanted to do for our country what our country had done for us, and our van was the first step in that direction.

"Together, we hauled dozens of children to Little League games. Together, we have taken 4,000 pounds of food to a local church for a food bank - every Thursday. Today was my first Thursday without her. Together, we helped those reeling from Hurricane Sandy. The memories are flooding in. Of course, most recently, she has taken me across the country to honor lives lost in tragedy.

"Over the last six years, we have made more than ten trips across this country to honor lives. This last trip alone, we helped almost ten people who needed car repairs. She has taken us all on this beautiful journey where together we have loved, served, helped, healed, and honored hundreds of people."

He told anyone who listened that he had no immediate plans to replace the van. Bessie was irreplaceable, but Tommy tried to look at the big picture. During an interview with a local news broadcast, he had a forgiving outlook about his van's exit from his life.

"If that van got taken and it helped someone in some way, shape, or form, and it was the last good thing it did, then that's the way it's supposed to end," he told the news crew.

For as God-fearing as Karla is, she hated Tommy's reaction to the heist, telling him, "Could you just be an asshole just once?"

"Karla," he said, "trust the process."

Tommy Maher might not be a fortune teller, but things somehow work out for him.

Three months after his van was unexpectedly ripped out of his life, he had an incredibly vivid dream that Ole Bessie was found and returned to him. In the dream, the van had been used to haul auto parts. It felt so real. When he awoke that morning at 3:30 a.m. for his unwavering gym routine, he looked outside toward the street, only to discover that reality was harsher than his subconscious fantasy. There was no van parked on the curb outside his home. His sadness had become more noticeable.

"Maybe she'll come back to us one day," Cindy sadly said after hearing about the dream, knowing it was hard to keep hope alive.

Feb 26, 2024

While sitting at a desk at the fire station, looking over documents, an unidentified phone number lit up Tommy's cell screen. It had been a week since that lifelike dream about Bessie's return.

He answered.

"Mr. Maher," a man who introduced himself as a Nassau County detective said, "your van has been found."

Tommy felt like he'd won the lottery a second time.

"You have my van?"

"It's pretty beat up, but we got it."

"Are you sure? How'd it happen?"

"A sanitation worker found it. The window is boarded up and...."

"I'm sorry," Tommy interrupted. "Did you say a sanitation worker found it? Did I hear that right? A sanitation worker?"

"Yes."

Tommy's smile couldn't be removed, almost like it was painted on. He worked for the New York City sanitation department for two decades, so this felt so fitting.

Bessie was lost but now found, and she'd taken a walk on the wild side — if only Tommy Maher's van could talk. For the three months that Bessie was under, shall we say, "new management," the van had a different life. She'd been spray-painted, a window smashed and the ignition was in shambles. The thieves, who were arrested, had been using Bessie to dump a multitude of items illegally (maybe even auto parts, but there's no real way of knowing). The "Pay It Forward" slogan was painted over with white paint, and a cardboard box held up by duct tape replaced the window.

Bessie was broken and beaten and in need of some serious TLC, but she finally came home where she belonged.

Trust the process.

CHAPTER 3

Jeff Dion

1982

Paulette Dion attended the University of North Carolina in Greensboro, where she was an award-winning member of the debate team and graduated in 1979 with a degree in communications. Soon after getting her degree (with honors, naturally), the country fell into a recession, and people were desperate for work. First, there was a brief recession in the first six months of 1980, followed by a more prolonged one in 1981 and 1982. The job market was undesirable, with unemployment peaking at nearly 10%.

Arby's, the fast-food chain known for championing roast beef, wasn't exactly where Paulette thought she'd be after four years of schooling, but she ended up liking the work and quickly found herself as a manager and on an upward trajectory within the company. Plus, Arby's was expanding so quickly that it opened a new store almost weekly in the United States. Suffice it to say the Beef 'n Cheddar, jamocha shakes and Horsey Sauce were taking the country by storm.

The overachiever that Paulette was, regional managers asked her to relocate to Atlanta to work at a flagship store known for testing products before they hit the broader market. When the chain first began in 1964, the menu was limited to just roast beef sandwiches, potato chips and soft drinks. Thanks to stores like the one Paulette was headed to — franchises that did research and development — items like Curly-Q Fries and chicken sandwiches became menu staples. It feels almost sacrilegious to think of Arby's without curly fries!

In early April 1982, three weeks before she began her new job, Paulette packed up her Volkswagen Rabbit, left North Carolina and headed for her new home, an apartment complex in Sandy Springs, a densely populated suburb of Atlanta. Peppered with coffee shops, parks and restaurants, Sandy Springs is safe and considered one of the best places to live in Georgia. The area, however, became somewhat notorious for a different reason years later. National and international media descended on the suburb in January 1997 after a Sandy Springs abortion clinic was bombed using nails and shrapnel. The bomber turned out to be Eric Rudolph, the same man who set off a bomb just six months prior during the 1996 Summer Olympics at Centennial Olympic Park. Rudolph held a place on the FBI's 10 Most Wanted List for five years. He was eventually caught in Murphy, North Carolina, in 2003, after a rookie police officer spotted him rummaging through a dumpster and suspected a burglary in progress.

New to the region, Paulette started finding her groove in Sandy Springs, which was rapidly expanding and beginning to catch the eyes of Fortune 500 companies, many of whom would eventually relocate there. Paulette adored her garden-style apartment. A bit of a hippy, the single-bedroom apartment was decorated with flowers, large macrame wall hangings, tapestry art and different hues of brown, her favorite color.

Although the unit didn't have a washer and dryer (very few homes did in those days), a laundry room was located on the ground level. It was annoying to lug her clothes and towels up and down the stairs, but it wasn't laborious. A bit of a night owl, as so many hospitality industry workers are, Paulette would often do laundry in the evening. More often than not, she was alone down there, but she also liked the peaceful solitude and the dryer's therapeutic humming. Plus, she had her pick of the litter of machines. Everyone had their favorite, and she was no different — she liked the third machine from the left.

Hardly noteworthy, the apartment building's laundry room was typical, as white, heavily used machines lined the walls. An area for folding clothes was nearby and rarely used. Water rings lightly stained some of the room's tables, and people regularly took their clothes home while forgetting to take their detergent boxes with them. The occasional wallet was seen left behind, and you could almost always inherit a stranded sock or hand towel that had been left behind. Fluorescent lights buzzed as if they were trying to attract mosquitoes. A small unfinished storage room sat beside the washing machines with no doorknob, only a deadbolt lock. The room was so unassuming that most residents disregarded it.

Seen as an unnecessary expense because of a lack of crime, security services had been discontinued months before Paulette moved there.

Around 11:30 p.m. on April 17, 1982, Paulette, wearing brown sandals, corduroy pants and a dark blue jogging suit top, headed to the laundry room to begin the mundane task of cleaning her clothes and work uniforms. Upon entering the room, she noticed the door to that nondescript storage area was curiously open. Peeking over from a few feet away, her arms wrapped around her laundry basket, Paulette saw debris covering the dirt floor and a man squatting there. The man had a large forehead, receding hairline, unkempt hair and a significant gap in the front of his teeth. He obviously hadn't seen a dentist in years and took little pride in his appearance. He looked dirty.

"You're not supposed to be here," Paulette, then 23, said matter-of-factly while removing linens from her laundry basket and placing them into the front loader. Don't let the short brown hair and wry smile fool you. Though she was diminutive — standing only 5'3" and weighing 90 pounds — Paulette could be stern and persuasive. Her fiancé loved to tell her that she was "full of piss and vinegar."

Unmoved, the man fell asleep, having no interest in arguing or stating his case for sheltering in the storage room. Bewildered but not scared, Paulette casually retreated to her apartment and hoped the man she saw in the storage room wouldn't be there when it was time to move her clothes to the dryer an hour later. He would be spooked and long gone, she hoped.

After the soaps and suds had done their job, Paulette returned to the laundry room to check on the status of her clean clothes. Entering, she looked at the storage area. The door was still open, and the dirty man was still there. This time, he wasn't as apathetic about the situation either. Without speaking, he quickly lunged at the unsuspecting Paulette. Overpowering her slim body, the assailant began beating Paulette with his closed fists. It happened so fast that she couldn't scream, at least not loud enough to be heard by a neighbor. She was pinned to the white tile floor and couldn't get away. Mounting Paulette, the man had no plans to stop the attack, as he strangled her and only yielded when his victim was no longer breathing.

Choking the life out of a human being should have been enough for this disgusting excuse for a man, but that's wishful thinking. Unsatisfied with his work, this intruder-turned-murderer reached into his jeans pocket and pulled out a rusty pocketknife. His heart pounding with disgusting excitement, he leaned into Paulette's lifeless body and pushed the sharp edge into her flesh. He made a small cut here and a small cut there until he had carved the date into her body.

On his knees, he closed the blade and stored it back in the pocket, but he rarely took his eyes off Paulette. The murder was quick, and the man knew he should be leaving, but he couldn't help himself. In his final act of deviancy, perhaps most disturbing of all, he loosened his belt, pulled down his pants and began masturbating on the warm corpse in front of him. When he was done sickeningly pleasuring himself, he casually left the laundry room, fleeing into the dark Sandy Springs evening.

He made no effort to clean up the scene or hide his crime.

1981

Jeff Dion never met an argument he didn't like.

While in 9th grade at South Florida's Nova High School, the sharp-witted 14-year-old took a debate class from teacher Rhoda Radow, a bit of a local legend in Broward County as her debate teams won numerous local, regional, and national titles. She was tough but fair. You could even say that Mrs. Radow was harder on her younger students, as she made anyone under 16 compete in a local optimist oratorical contest.

These contests were designed to test students' abilities by providing them with a general topic to discuss and debate. The topics were often cheesy and made little sense, which was by design and part of the challenge.

After enrolling in the class, Jeff knew what he was in for, given that his older sister, Paulette, also took debate classes from Mrs. Radow. As someone under 16, all he had to do was await whatever nebulous topic he'd have to discuss at the oratorical contest.

He was ready with a pencil in hand when Mrs. Radow finally announced the topic in class.

"Your topic is You and I and Tomorrow."

Huh? What. Does. That. Mean.

Dozens of kids raised their hands for clarification.

"Part of the exercise is figuring out what that means," she said after noticing the deer-in-headlights looks from the barely teenage students. "You need to think critically and be resourceful."

Luckily for Jeff, his teacher knew which buttons to push and which levers to pull to get him to think creatively and make convincing arguments. Mrs. Radow was something of a debating sovereign.

A brilliant student, Jeff was sharp enough to get by in his classes with minimal studying. His grades would have been higher had he just done the homework, but he always procrastinated until he was up against a deadline, and the oratorical contest was no different. Sitting in front of the television on the eve of the contest, Jeff wrote his speech on white notecards.

The following day, the Nova High freshman cooly got on stage and discussed how today's decisions shape the future and how those decisions must be made with an eye toward long-term goals. He impressed the judges and came in second place, quite a feat for someone whose hobbies included collecting comic books and earning Boy Scout merit badges.

Wanting to brag a bit, he couldn't wait to phone Paulette, who had just moved to Atlanta for a job opportunity with the fast-food chain.

"I got second place!" Jeff crowed to his sister, who could hear the excitement in his voice. Paulette, a few years into adulthood, was immensely proud of her baby brother and encouraged him to stick with it. She was his biggest cheerleader and always felt he was destined for great things. Letting her sibling have his moment, she didn't remind him that she took first place in that same oratorical contest.

When Jeff hung up the phone that day, he didn't know that it would be the last time he would ever speak to his sister. She was deeply supportive of her brother until the end. Literally.

April 18, 1982

Paulette was supposed to report to her job at Arby's this morning, but she never showed up. An exemplary employee, this wasn't normal. She was always either on time or early. This was long before cell phones were commonplace, so her confused coworkers began phoning her landline incessantly. No one was answering.

Ring, ring, ring.

This was so out of character for the professionally minded Paulette.

Endless ringing and ringing and ringing eventually led to a phone call to the police for a welfare check.

Around the time Paulette's home was deluged with calls, all coming from Arby's coworkers, an unsuspecting neighbor descended to the laundry room to do a simple load on a Sunday morning, utterly oblivious to the horror that had happened hours earlier.

As the neighbor entered the laundry room, the lights were on, but a machine wasn't running, so he assumed no one was doing laundry that early. He first noticed two laundry baskets stacked on top of one of the machines, but then saw an image he'd never forget: Paulette's nude, lifeless body lying on the floor in a pool of firm blood.

Because the Arby's team had already contacted the police for the welfare check, they were already on their way when the neighbor's frantic 911 call came through.

The youngest of four Dion kids, Jeff and his older brother, Greg, were working at a church carnival hawking hot dogs, hamburgers and Italian sausages when his solemn-faced father broke the Paulette news to them. Jeff wanted to talk about it immediately, but his dad stayed tight-lipped. In moments, his feelings washed over him in different waves: first, shock and disbelief, followed by crippling grief, and finally anger. This did not just occur out of happenstance.

Someone did this to her. He hoped it was just a bad dream. The worst dream.

As his father had not shared the gruesome details, Jeff found out how his sister died when a neighbor handed him a newspaper article. Reading it, he felt detached. The article seemed no different than countless other crime articles he had read over the years, and he thought, "There's no way this is my sister they're talking about." He suddenly realized that for each of those previous articles he had read without a second thought, there was a family left behind whose world had been completely turned upside down.

Jeff felt like he was sleepwalking for weeks. After his parents retrieved Paulette's property from her apartment and brought it home to South Florida, the precocious teen started looking through cardboard boxes of his sister's belongings. While sifting through clothes, hairbrushes, books and knick-knacks, he came across the 1974 speech that netted her a win in the oratorical contest (the one he took second place in). The topic was "I'm Just One." Getting emotional, Jeff read as Paulette spoke about the difference one person can make for good or evil. She cited Adolf Hitler (evil), Martin Luther King Jr. and Cesar Chavez (both good).

Jeff read his sister's words while sitting cross-legged on his bedroom floor: "Everyone has the right to dream. Everyone has the duty to aid mankind, and everyone has the opportunity to try to change the world."

Stunned and shaking, Jeff knew that this speech and these words were his sister's lasting gift to him. The speech might as well have been her way of taking him by the hand and guiding him. He knew then that he wouldn't rest until he knew the details of his sister's death, even the grisly parts. No detail was too small.

Having obtained the address of the Atlanta Police Department, Jeff, still just 14 years old, penned a letter to the police chief requesting a copy of the police report and any other available information. This wasn't cold calling, per se, but rather cold lettering. Not realizing it at the time, but that letter became his first act of victim advocacy, something he would dedicate his life to.

Weeks passed until Jeff received a response from the police, a denial of his request. In a moment of adolescent fantasy, he thought, "If they haven't caught Paulette's murderer by the time I'm out of high school, I'll go find him."

1984

Jeff's delusions of vigilante justice didn't come to fruition, however, because police ultimately arrested a man for the murder, something the teen was told while being driven by his mother to an orthodontist appointment.

"The police called today, and Paulette's killer has confessed."

The murderer had actually been in police custody for a year before admitting to Paulette's heinous killing. Following a brief pause, Jeff's mom added, "You're never going to guess who it is."

For a split second, Jeff, now 16, prayed, "Please don't tell me I know this person!"

"It was Toole."

Sitting silently as the South Florida scenery scrolled past him in the passenger window, Jeff wondered why and how he knew that name. It then came to him: Ottis Toole was a drifter and one of the most notorious serial killers in the country, having been linked to the kidnapping and murder of 6-year-old Adam Walsh, the son of "America's Most Wanted" host John Walsh.

Adam's abduction had captured the interest of the country, as the tot was taken from the Hollywood Mall in Hollywood, Florida, on July 27, 1981, while shopping with his mother. Jeff grew up four miles from the mall and saw posters of

Adam's face on every pillar and post in South Florida. Everyone in the area was aware of the abduction. For two weeks, the Walsh family pleaded and prayed and even offered a $100,000 reward for Adam's safe return. However, the Walsh family's worst fears were realized when the young boy's severed head was found in a drainage ditch 130 miles from Hollywood on August 10.

Toole, as he was often referred to, later equated his killings to smoking cigarettes, saying it was just a habit. Cold and callous in his descriptions, he was convicted of five murders, but he was never charged or even tried in court for so many of his other murders, including Paulette's.

"He's been convicted five times of first-degree murder, so it serves no public purpose to go through with a trial," an attorney told Jeff.

More than a decade later, Jeff actually met John Walsh at a police-sponsored Crime Victims' Rights Week Commemoration, and the two discussed their family members' cases. In that meeting, the TV host erased all doubt in Jeff's mind that Toole was indeed the man responsible for his sister's death. Jeff never could have imagined that the same man who killed little Adam Walsh was also responsible for murdering his sister.

He was truly a sick individual.

Just before tragically murdering Paulette, Toole killed a 64-year-old man with whom he was having a sexual relationship by locking the man inside his own home and lighting it on fire. He later met up with another sexual companion, a homicidal lunatic named Henry Lee Lucas, and the men murdered and committed violent crimes at will. This was their hobby. Most people play cards, sew or read. These two casually killed.

After their arrests, both men confessed to hundreds of murders but later recanted their confessions. The true number of the killings isn't known, seeing that they muddied the waters with their unlimited murder admissions.

For Toole, crime was a means to an end, claiming he was a prostitute at the age of 10. Growing up in a home littered with incest and sexual abuse, he often ran away and slept in abandoned houses. Sometimes, he would torch the home — you know, just because he could. At 14, his crimes graduated to murder, as it's believed he killed a traveling salesman by intentionally running him over with a car — again, just because he could.

Despite Toole's low IQ and learning disabilities, he was able to largely evade police for nearly two decades.

Still, Jeff's desire to find out everything about Paulette's death was of profound importance, but he discovered that the police department didn't have a single victim's advocate to tell families what their rights were. Nobody was feeding the Dion family information. They were on their own. Having realized the chief of police wasn't exactly forthcoming and didn't want to be a pen pal, Jeff contacted a lawyer he knew — a Boy Scout leader named Andy Grayson — and asked him to call police for not only Paulette's records but also those of Toole, who was confessing to an endless amount of murders from a Jacksonville jail cell.

"Jeff, there's not going to be a trial, but you don't have to worry. Toole is never going to get out of jail. He's killed far too many people," the lawyer asserted. "A lot of police want to speak to him. Even the Atlanta cops had to wait for six hours for their turn to talk to him."

"This is my sister!" an unfulfilled Jeff internally screamed. "Why do we have to wait for everyone else? Where are our answers! Where's our justice!"

There was little doubt that Toole killed Paulette, as semen left on her body was linked to him via an enzyme secretion test, a way of tying suspects to a scene in the pre-DNA days.

Still, Jeff was angry, somber and disheartened. That feeling of having to wallow in mystery and, to an extent, misery left a lasting impression, so much so that he dedicated his life to making things right, having decided the best way to honor his sister was to become a victim's right lawyer and support those who've suffered the worst kind of loss.

His decision to become a lawyer was also aided and supported by a man who would become the President of the United States a few decades later.

Being a voice for victims is Jeff's life's work, and he's hard to stop when he sets his mind to something. Over the years, he has consistently lobbied the Virginia General Assembly and successfully enacted 13 victims' rights bills into law.

Along the way, he also established the nonprofit Mass Violence Survivors Fund, a transparent mechanism for collecting and distributing charitable contributions in the aftermath of mass violence. Jeff and his team are usually the first call local governments make when setting up official GoFundMe accounts for victims and survivors of mass casualty events. His organization handles the funds, creates the protocol, verifies victims and distributes money. Every dollar raised is tracked, and 100% of it goes to the verified survivors and their families. The team behind the funds, who doesn't take a dime of it, works diligently to find a major sponsor to cover their administrative costs, leaving all the raised money to go to those who suffered loss or injury due to a mass casualty incident.

After the Las Vegas shooting in 2017, more than 90,000 donors from all over the world contributed more than $32 million to the fund, and it was distributed among the 515 beneficiaries, victims, survivors, and families. The GoFundMe funds differ from the insurance payouts that may occur simultaneously.

At this point, the Fund is a bit of a turn-key operation tailored to the specific event. Jeff and his team were at the forefront of assisting family members and administering GoFundMe money after the mass shootings at Orlando's Pulse Nightclub, Marjory Stoneman Douglas High School in Parkland, Florida, Tops supermarket in Buffalo, New York, Robb Elementary School in Uvalde, Texas, a FedEx

Ground facility in Indianapolis, Indiana, and yes, Las Vegas' Route 91 rampage, which is how Mary Jo met him. He has the best interests of the survivors in mind, both emotionally and financially.

Through this work as a victim's advocate, Jeff has administered 30 different relief funds for mass casualty events and has collected and distributed over $150 million for victims via the nonprofit.

"There's a lot of isolation to victimization, and it is so different from any other realm of the human experience," he notes. "When I work with survivors of mass casualty crimes, I explain who I am and why I do it. I haven't walked in their shoes, but something similar happened to me. I think that gives us some credibility with those survivors, and it helps us to do that work. Survivors know that we get it."

Not to be hyperbolic, but Jeff Dion might be the most trauma-informed man in the country. Still, he's never lost sight of his purpose.

"He's still fighting for Paulette," said longtime friend and respected wrongful death attorney Marc Lenahan, who ended up helping Jeff home in on his message when dealing with groups.

The way Marc tells it, he once watched his pal speak at a conference in Oregon. It was nearing the end of a very long day when Jeff finally mentioned his sister. In journalism, there's a saying called "burying the lead," meaning stories should begin with the most interesting, compelling or shocking information. Marc felt Jeff was burying the lead, but the Texas-based attorney described it more eloquently, echoing a message he had once heard from a popular pastor. In the sermon, pastor T.D. Jakes spoke about Jesus walking into a room full of disciples after the crucifixion. No one batted an eye. Jesus then lifted his shirt to show the holes on his side. He followed by showing the holes in his hands. The disciples rushed to embrace Jesus.

"Before somebody hears your message, you need to show them your wounds," said Marc, who's religiously indifferent. "Showing them your wounds opens the door to letting them hear what you have to say. I told that exact same thing to Jeff."

Soon after, Jeff would open his lectures by speaking about his late sister. To this day, he mentions Paulette in his opening monologue.

"It's important for everybody in the room to know that he's there because he's fighting for her still," Marc said.

To college basketball fans, George Mason University was the little engine that could in the 2006 NCAA Tournament. The Patriots entered the tournament as an 11 seed, meaning not much was thought of them. Coached by Jim Larrañaga, the team upset perennial title contender Michigan State in the first round. With nary an NBA player among them, the team from Northern Virginia took down blue bloods North Carolina and Connecticut before finally succumbing to eventual national champion Florida. At the time, they matched the record for the lowest seed ever to reach the Final Four.

That magical run — which ESPN called "the greatest in NCAA Tournament history" — thrust underdog George Mason into national consciousness and, to sports junkies, put the school on the map. Outside of the athletic world, George Mason is more known for its research in the health field. Its law school is well-regarded, and alumni have included politicians and presidential advisors.

Jeff Dion had no ties to the Virginia area while looking at college acceptance letters, but he liked the idea of attending a school located a stone's throw from Washington, D.C.'s legislators. Always politically minded, he considered contacting congressmen about various issues over the years, but that wasn't always plausible. Plus, it was expensive. Back then, long-distance phone calls cost money, so they were done sparingly. In Virginia, though, he was astounded to discover that a call to the Nation's Capital was local and free. After all, the White House was only 20 miles away. Marathoners run longer distances than that.

When Jeff arrived as a freshman at George Mason, he knew he was close to the political epicenter of the country, particularly given that the campus had been inundated with campaign posters for Republican gubernatorial hopeful Wyatt Durrett, a U.S. Air Force veteran who was then working as a lawyer. The fact that Durrett signs were everywhere wasn't surprising, as Fairfax County was a staunch Republican stronghold. The GOP presidential candidate had taken the county vote in all but one election from 1944 to 2000. It wasn't until the turn of the century that Fairfax flipped blue.

Whether it was on billboards adjacent to campus or on the front lawn of the student union building, Durrett signs were everywhere.

"Where are the Democrats?" Jeff wondered that fall day in 1985 while strolling the scenic campus, which sits on 677 wooded acres. The foliage was changing colors, and the college freshman thought the campus's political leaning could, too.

Like he did when he wanted answers from the police about his sister's murder, Jeff took matters into his own hands, perusing the Yellow Pages for the Democratic National Committee's phone number. The DNC was based in D.C., therefore, a local phone number —a free phone call.

"We need a Young Democrats Club out here at George Mason," he told a middle-ranking DNC worker.

"Great idea," the person on the other end retorted. "Go start one."

Ever driven, Jeff did just that, but he also wanted the new club to make a splash. During the creation of George

Mason's Young Democrats Club, Jeff had been reading extensively about a junior senator from Delaware named Joe Biden. The epiphany came to him: He should call Joe Biden's office and get the lawmaker to speak on campus. Jeff was fearless, prepared and ready to convince this up-and-coming senator to come to his campus. Besides, national political organizations were projecting big things from this Biden guy. At 43 years old, Biden had the charisma, wits, respect of his peers and a heartbreaking backstory, as his wife and 1-year-old daughter both died in a car crash six weeks after he was elected to the Senate.

On March 4, 1987, three-term senator Joe Biden arrived 30 minutes late at George Mason to speak on international foreign policy. It was Ash Wednesday. Jeff actually introduced the then-senator, future president, calling him an "expert on foreign policy" and an "outstanding orator."

As a handwritten poster welcoming the senator hung behind a dais, Jeff passionately and eloquently boasted about Biden in an introduction that would have made Winston Churchill applaud. It was determined, informative and inspirational. It was, well, a persuasive political speech.

"Franklin Roosevelt's New Deal put this country back on its feet. John Kennedy's New Frontier inspired us to explore new areas of science and space. Let Joe Biden's new generation remind us all that despite our vast array of wealth and technology, we can do better. We must move forward."

Yes, Jeff can speak. He has a gift. Aside from Biden's tardiness, which was out of Jeff's control, he had every "i" dotted and every "t" crossed for this day.

Perhaps either feeling upstaged or wondering if he'd just met the future of the Democratic party, Biden took the dais and didn't hide his impression of Jeff, having only met him for a few seconds.

"I learned a long time ago there are several things a public speaker should not do," Biden said. "One is keeping his audience waiting. Two, stand between his audience and a meal. And three, follow a young man or woman who is a better orator. I think I have just violated all three rules, and I'd like to begin by complimenting Jeff, who obviously has no interest in politics, for that very gracious introduction."

Jeff sat there stunned as this mammoth of a political figure publicly recognized him in that way. Joe Biden had called him out by name and had given him his just due as an orator. He was gobsmacked. Jeff's knees were like Jello, and Biden had Jeff in the palm of his hand. A video of the speech can still be seen on YouTube today.

Biden, who was not-so-secretly gearing up for a run at the White House, was personally impressed with Jeff, as was his team. Because of his tenacity in getting the popular senator to George Mason and setting up all the behind-the-scenes logistics, Jeff was offered a job on Biden's campaign staff, which he happily accepted, even though he was still working his way through his undergrad degree. Jeff was absolutely convinced he was about to work with the future President of the United States, and he was right — just 32 years early.

Biden's 1988 campaign was short-lived after being dogged by plagiarism accusations, but the future vice president had a Christmas party at his house for the campaign staff to thank them of their work. Surrounded by tinsel, wrapped presents, a beautiful Christmas tree and an open bar, Biden sought Jeff out.

"Jeff, come here," he said. "I think you should pursue law school. It's a very practical consideration because lawyers often get to control their own schedules. It takes a lot of time and you've got to have some flexibility."

Before diving headfirst into politics, Biden had been a lawyer and saw much of himself in Jeff.

"If you want to run for office, you should be a lawyer," the 46th President of the United States urged.

That did it. Jeff had already thought that becoming an attorney would be a possible career path, but it was Joe Biden who convinced him to apply to law school (he did and was accepted). After that pivotal evening, Jeff continued to work on Democratic campaigns throughout college and donated his time to both local and national efforts.

Through his experience on political campaigns, Jeff learned the value of structure and resolution, which served him well in organizing and building nonprofits for mass casualty incidents. Oddly, there are some similarities: people donate to campaigns as they do mass casualty funds; political campaigns use the press as a tool, as do mass casualty events.

Say what you will, but he has a complex skill set.

Spurred by his sister's murder, Jeff knew his legal passion was victims' rights, but jobs weren't being handed out on a silver platter. He unsuccessfully applied for positions in several prosecutors' offices but soon found work with a civil litigation firm. While there, the National Center for Victims of Crime had an opening for a lawyer with a background in victims' rights and civil litigation and contacted Jeff. It was a perfect fit for his skills. The gig would help define Jeff, and he swiftly became a feared adversary to those skirting the law. In time, he would help bring down Catholic leaders or Boy Scout figureheads who assaulted children by increasing the statute of limitations for sex abuse; he went after security officers who exhibited negligence; he zeroed in on bars for over-serving drunk drivers who later killed someone on roadways; he was also a driving force to get truth-in-sentencing laws changed in Virginia — felons must serve at least 85% of the incarceration sentence, something that wasn't happening until Jeff got involved; and, of course, he got those 13 victim's rights bills enacted into law in Virginia.

Before Jeff's involvement, Virginia had been one of only two states that limited victim impact statements to the written word. Under a new law, survivors could offer oral impact testimony during the sentencing phase of a trial. Surviving members of homicide victims have rights because of Jeff

Dion's lobbying. They can now speak in court about the impact of the crime and make sure their loved one isn't just another statistic. Families could look judges and perpetrators in the eye and show visible emotional pain. Thankfully, the vast majority of the public won't ever be affected by this law change, but it was beyond a blessing for grieving family members.

For the first time, family members could fight for their loved ones and prevent them from being overlooked. Homicides affect so many more people than just the deceased, and Jeff made sure surviving relatives had a seat at the table.

Knowing firsthand the pain that comes from losing someone to crime, he was somewhat of a mouthpiece for scarred families, and his actions spoke louder than his words.

"I used to joke with him that nobody puts baby in the corner because he never shuts up," said Carroll Anne Ellis, alluding to the famous "Dirty Dancing" quote.

The Director of Victim Services at Fairfax County Police Department, Carroll remembers meeting Jeff in the early '90s when he attended a support group for homicide survivors (the term used for families of homicide victims). Carroll is a luminary in police circles and among homicide survivors. A psychologist by trade, she provided support for homicide survivors after 9/11, after the D.C. sniper attacks of 2002 and after the CIA shootings of 1993. Some of her career is chronicled in John Douglas and Mark Olshaker's 1998 book *Obsession.* There, the authors describe her as a "proverbial fish out of water — a civilian in a police world, a woman in a man's world, a black in a white suburban world." They also note that many homicide survivors credit Carroll for making it possible to continue with their lives. Carroll is somehow able to be commanding and still be an acute listener. She's compassionate and empathic. Her message to the family of homicide victims is simple: We hear you, we see you, you are not forgotten and we're here to help you. She often says,

"Everything that I know about homicide I learned from a homicide survivor."

In 2007, Carroll was a constant presence on C-Span after then-Virginia Governor Tim Kaine asked her to serve on the Virginia Tech Incident Review Panel, which was put together after an undergraduate student killed 32 people and wounded 17 others during a shooting at the Blacksburg, Virginia, campus on April 16, 2007. For four months, she spoke with surviving family members of victims and heard all about their heartaches and pains. She assisted first responders who wouldn't forget the images of the massacre and worked with media members whose lives suddenly revolved around mass deaths. It wasn't uncommon for first responders to fall asleep thinking about the Virginia Tech shooting and wake up thinking about it. It was consuming. Carroll is somewhat of a release valve for survivors who need to sound off after mental pressure builds.

Carroll was impressed when she first met Jeff in 1995. At the time, he was a young lawyer and would sometimes attend the meetings with his infant son in his arms. He told everyone about his sister's death, which gave him a sense of belonging in the group.

"He was a little lawyer full of energy and willing to talk. He was very, very effective in the group," Carroll said. "He spoke out, and he had good, solid information based on his education as far as law is concerned."

Looking back, Jeff sheepishly admits that he attended his first meeting "rather pompously," thinking he could help these people because of his legal education. Instead, though, Jeff was shell-shocked after entering the room. There was a woman whose mother was murdered. There was a man whose sister was murdered. Another person's daughter was killed. It was the very first time Jeff had ever met another person who'd lost a loved one to homicide.

In this group setting, everyone would go around the room sharing their stories, while others would discuss their grievances with the criminal justice system. Jeff, a lawyer, would occasionally explain the law. But sometimes, he couldn't explain why things were the way they were. Ever diligent, he bookmarked these moments and later fought to change laws to be more favorable to homicide survivors. The vast majority of those 13 aforementioned law changes stemmed from this group environment.

It was at Carroll's meetings that Jeff met homicide survivor John Walsh. Other homicide survivors invited to speak to the support group included Ron Goldman, whose son was killed in 1994 alongside OJ Simpson's ex-wife Nicole Brown Simpson, Michael Jordan, whose father was killed while napping in a car, and Bill Cosby, whose son was murdered while changing a tire on the side of the road. The latter two never attended any of Carroll's meetings.

For 20 years, Carroll spearheaded the support group, and she soon came to rely on Jeff to empathize with survivors. His credibility with the support group grew because, as Marc Lenahan said, he showed people his wounds. Paulette's name was alive and well within the group. Jeff was understanding, used eloquent wording to speak to fellow survivors and would talk about what helped his healing, which included getting over the hatred he felt for his sister's killer.

Jeff talked and talked and talked.

Nobody puts baby in the corner.

On September 12, 2001, the world was still reeling from the ghastly terrorist attacks that took place. As the death toll in New York, Washington, D.C. and Pennsylvania's Somerset County continued to rise, airline lobbyists descended on Capitol Hill with hopes to grant immunity to American and United, the two companies that saw their planes being used as weapons the previous day.

Enter Jeff Dion.

As part of his job as a victim's advocate with the National Center for Victims of Crime, Jeff wanted survivors and victims' families to know they were entitled to financial compensation from a government fund created for the deaths that happened on 9/11. But, to get money from the fund, survivors had to waive their right to sue the airlines or the government. Additionally, information about the attack would be withheld.

Throughout 27 forums, Jeff met thousands of survivors and victims' families. He told them that non-litigious people had a claim to a government compensation fund. Jeff worked with 1,500 victims and surviving family members to help them understand their rights. Ultimately, about 90% of the 9/11 survivors opted for the fund. The other 10% of the survivors and their families weren't necessarily interested in pursuing further compensation through a lawsuit, but rather in obtaining information. It was because of these 10% that videos of the airplane hijackers going through airport security screenings came into public consciousness.

"Jeff is an insanely diligent micromanager," said Marc Lenahan, who sat on the National Crime Victims Bar Association board with Jeff. "He really leaves no stone unturned. He really thinks about everything in advance."

Colorado changed everything.

Following the Aurora, Colorado, movie theater shooting in 2012, which saw 12 deaths and 70 others injured, survivors were not satisfied with the charitable fund that had been established, and Jeff was asked to set up a new fund for them — his reputation had obviously preceded him. Realizing that these crimes were unfortunately not stopping, the trauma-minded Jeff began building an infrastructure to allow for immediate charitable donations to help victims in the wake of mass casualty events. Before the Aurora shooting, other funds had certainly been created, but psychologically traumatized victims were left out. Money only went to those physically hurt, but Jeff was aware that victims could certainly be negatively affected mentally by mass casualty events, too, they were included via a sliding scale under the new format. The new infrastructure, which became the National Compassion Fund and was later changed to the Mass Violence Survivors Fund, has since been used following shootings in Fort Hood, Texas, El Paso, Texas, and Chattanooga, Tennessee, among others. Jeff helped administer these relief funds to ensure survivors weren't left out to dry.

Amy Franco was a recipient of a fund that Jeff distributed, and she doesn't know where she'd be without it.

A 23-year employee of Uvalde Consolidated Independent School District, Amy was a new employee at Robb Elementary School in Uvalde, Texas, on May 24, 2022, having only started her position as the coordinator of ACE, an afterschool program for students, one month prior. While preparing for her day in room 132, a room plastered with pictures drawn by students and adjacent to Robb's west entrance, Amy munched on a peanut butter and jelly sandwich and sipped her coffee. Much of that day's preparation centered on the following day, wherein ACE planned a dance to commemorate the end of another school year. The revelry was going to have all the bells and whistles, including a popcorn machine, pickle stand and nacho bar — everything elementary kids love. A carnival vibe was expected. While going over the balance sheet, Amy's phone rang. It was a colleague with a carload of pizzas, which would be reheated the following day.

"Can you open the back gate so we don't have to walk these through the front door?" he said, his car practically oozing marinara and mozzarella.

"I'll be right there."

After walking out of her classroom, Amy made an immediate right, putting her in front of the school's west doors, which are opened via a three-foot-long push bar.

Knowing the pizza run would require multiple runs and wanting to make things more efficient, she opened the door and kept it ajar with a reasonably large rock. While walking toward the pie-filled car, the otherwise quiet afternoon was suddenly filled with the sound of an out-of-control truck revving its engine, crashing into an adjacent guardrail and settling in a ditch about 100 yards from Robb, a school located about 60 miles from the Mexican border. Surely, this was a terrible accident, she assumed.

Taken aback, Amy ran back to her classroom, grabbed her phone and dialed 911 to report the emergency, believing the driver needed help. The pizzas could wait an extra minute or two. While on the phone with a 911 operator, Amy went back outside, the rock still propping the door open, and briskly walked toward the black 2008 Ford F-150 to assist with the rescue efforts.

"A truck just crashed outside Robb Elementary. I think someone's hurt," he told the operator, who was dispatching emergency services.

While staying on with the 911 operator and continuing her march toward the ditch, Amy saw two nicely dressed men from the nearby Hillcrest Memorial Funeral Home walking toward the scene to help, as well. Her head cocked slightly to the side as those same two good Samaritans stopped on a dime, turned around and started sprinting away, looking terrified.

"He's got a gun. He's got a gun!" they screamed.

Once again, that quiet day was being interrupted, this time by hollow-point bullets being fired at the two funeral home workers by the man who'd just crashed the truck. The men stumbled to the ground to avoid the bullets.

Pop, pop, pop, pop... Pop, pop, pop, pop...

Immediately realizing what was happening, the ACE coordinator quickly reversed course, turned around and made a mad dash for the school, knowing she had to outrun the gunfire to warn others. She also had to kick that damn rock out from the door.

While running as fast as her petite frame would allow, the gunman, holding an AR-15 style rifle and wearing a tactical vest, scaled a five-foot-tall exterior fence and took a direct route toward Robb's entry doors while unloading his clip. To this day, Amy doesn't know if the gunman was firing at her, but she had no plans to turn around to find out.

"Oh my God, oh my God," she said while losing breath and running as close as she could get to Olympic speeds.

Getting back to the west entrance of Robb Elementary, she momentarily paused, cocked her right leg back and thrust it forward, using her foot to kick the rock far out of the way. Stepping a few feet inside, she desperately pulled the door closed and assumed it had locked.

"Get in your rooms!" she shouted at curious kids who heard the car crash and the ensuing popping of, maybe, fireworks.

Still giving the 911 operator a play-by-play — a call later released to the public — she retreated to her classroom, the very first classroom when entering from Robb's west side. The panic in her voice is unmistakable and gut-wrenching.

"Where are the cops?" she demanded to know as she listened intently to gunfire, but still devoid of any police sirens. With the sound of gunfire speeding up, her connection went dead, and she wondered if she, too, would suffer the same fate as her cell phone.

Crouched on her toes under a countertop in her student-less room, Amy knew the situation was dicey, but she was absolutely confident she had closed the outer door, which was designed to automatically lock after being shut. She would soon find out that, through no fault of her own, the door was faulty, and it didn't lock, making the gunman's 11:33 a.m. entry too easy.

The gunman, an 18-year-old former Robb student who shot his grandmother earlier that day, fatally shot 19 students and two teachers in adjoining classrooms 111 and 112. School surveillance video shows him bypassing Amy's room, veering right, walking a short distance and opening fire on the connected rooms. Most of his over 100 rounds were fired before officers arrived three minutes later.

Although officers initially ran toward the classroom, they soon fell back. For the next 74 minutes, local law enforcement huddled in the hallway right outside Amy's door. The school was so eerily quiet that she could hear their hushed conversations. Fearing so much for her life, she didn't move. Despite every instinct in her body telling her to scream, cry or even run, she didn't want to make a single sound. For 45 minutes, she was crouched down, her entire body tilted forward, only being held up by her 10 curled toes. The strain was debilitating while waiting for police to give the "all clear." Had she been able to stay in that position for 74 minutes, she would have, but the pain was too much. She finally sat down. Her toes were somehow numb and tortuously throbbing. Amy was eventually diagnosed with post-traumatic arthritis, which came as a result of being stuck in that unnatural position on her toes for so long.

For days, she was emotionally, spiritually and physically in pain. Things, though, would get worse after police claimed that a school employee left the west side door propped open with a rock. Amy was actually being publicly blamed but was eventually exonerated of wrongdoing. In fact, the 911 call displayed her heroism as she implored the kids to return to their rooms, and surveillance video clearly showed her kicking out the rock and closing the door. However, she was vilified in her small, rural community. Suffering from psychological pain and survivor's guilt, she didn't leave her house for weeks. Even after authorities publicly cleared Amy, no school district member bothered to check on her well-being. Likewise, no one ever apologized for falsely accusing her of essentially rolling out the red carpet for the shooter.

Uvalde County is large in size, but the actual city of Uvalde, the county seat, carries a population of merely 15,000. More than half of its residents are Hispanic, and everyone seems to know everyone. Rodeos are common, farms stretch as far as the eye can see and most people are bilingual (as evidenced by Robb Elementary School's welcome sign reading "Welcome" and "Bienvenido.") Prior to the school shooting, the town was known for being the "Honey Capitol of the World" and the birthplace of Oscar winner Matthew McConaughey.

Amy had always loved Uvalde and felt at peace there, but she felt like an outsider post-Robb because of the brief slander thrown her way.

One month following the shooting, she heard about a survivor's fund being distributed by a man she'd never heard of. His name, Jeffrey Dion, meant nothing to her, and she feared that she'd be treated like another statistic. She was pretty sure that her story would be dismissed because she wasn't shot that day, she didn't break any bones, nor was she in classrooms 111, 112 or 109, a third room part of the crime scene. Other than investigators, few people stepped foot in that school ever again, and it's set to be demolished.

Her emotional scars were still fresh when Amy first saw Jeff at the neighborhood civic center. Clad in a pressed suit, subtle wire-rimmed glasses and perfectly combed coif, she thought he was very handsome. Within moments, she was drawn to his heart and compassion.

"He actually listened to me," she said. "He was actually trying to help."

With precise detail, Jeff told Amy that she qualified for a fund that had been established. Her injuries, caused by her body position during the shooting, made her eligible for additional funding, too. After being the subject of false accusations and unsympathetic neighbors and colleagues, Jeff was a blessing to Amy at a time when the community was failing her.

In a previous life, Amy was a happy-go-lucky optimist, but she now suffers from PTSD. She shakes often, takes medication for anxiety, struggles with loud sounds and no longer works. She's finding solace in painting these days. It's therapeutic. It allows her to avoid specific triggers since she stays in the safe confines of home, and, well, it brightens the walls of her apartment.

Six months after the shooting, Amy received financial compensation from the $22 million fund that Jeff Dion administered.

"Without Jeff, I'd be much worse than I am. I don't know where I'd be without Jeff," she said. "He even sends me a Christmas card every year."

Psychological trauma, like what Amy suffered, is incredibly hard to quantify, but Jeff has experience there. Too much experience, actually.

Following the June 12, 2016, shooting at Pulse Nightclub in Orlando, Jeff and the National Center for Victims of Crime tried to weigh people's psychological trauma based on how long they were trapped in the prominent gay club, so his team set up an open space to allow victims to write in and share their experiences.

He read every single one of the survivors' written statements.

Wrote one man in the open space, "I am crawling on my hands and knees towards the door of the club, and I'm pretty much convinced that I'm going to die. And I'm okay with that, but all I could think of is, this is how my parents find out I'm gay."

He helped oversee and distribute every penny of $33.6 million in donations to survivors and families after Pulse.

Shoes became a vivid memory for Jeff in the wake of the school shooting at Oxford High School just outside of Michigan. When a student began opening fire in a hallway, killing four and injuring nine, kids ran for their lives, so much so that many of them lost their footwear in the process. When police entered the building, long hallways were scattered with shoes. "My son always double knots his shoes now because he saw so many people literally jump out of their shoes," one mother wrote in a letter to Jeff of her son, who survived the Oxford shooting.

In every fund, those who experienced psychological trauma are always considered both victims and survivors. Jeff also works with a local steering committee in each area, allowing them to avoid pitfalls.

"I carry all of these things from all of these people with me, and I worry that we have become desensitized," Jeff told me.

Following the Vegas shooting, Jeff was in charge of administering the survivors' fund, which was set up by Steve Sisolak and Joe Lombardo, two men who eventually became Nevada's Governor (they even ran against each other in 2022 — Lombardo won, beating incumbent Sisolak). There, survivors and the families of victims were assigned a level of benefit based on their experiences. A publicly available chart showed that $275,000 was paid to the families of the 58 people killed. Ten others who were paralyzed or suffered permanent brain damage got the same payout. A sliding scale determined how much others would get. Mary Jo's first knowledge of Jeff came when he hosted a town hall in Vegas to discuss how the funds would be distributed.

"He was confident, well-spoken, concise and ready for all the emotions of the families. There were some real moments of contention," Mary Jo said. "I attended via Zoom, but Jeff was impressive, even through a computer screen."

Over time, she developed a relationship with Jeff and his staff at the nonprofit, and he actually asked her to speak at a conference for victims of crime in Orlando in front of 1,200 people, to which she agreed. Other speakers included survivors from Marjory Stoneman Douglas High School and Pulse Nightclub.

Unbeknownst to her, Jeff was also flying to Sacramento the following day, so they arranged to sit next to each other while airborne. There, throughout the five-hour flight, Mary Jo learned about his sister.

"Seeing him flourish after experiencing something so tragic inspired me and gave me hope that I could also make something good out of my own terrible situation," she said.

Spurred by Jeff and others entering her trauma-filled orbit, Mary Jo was determined to make something positive from her husband's murder.

"I'd like to think my speaking gigs made a difference in people's lives. I know they made a difference in mine."

In late 2023, Jeff started a new victims fund that does the same work he'd been doing, but this one was called the Mass Violence Survivors Fund. It's comprised of four staff members and five mass casualty survivors, including Mary Jo. Jeff is the Executive Director, whereas she serves as treasurer on the board of directors. Similar to the National Guard, they are only activated as needed. In reality, they hope they never have to be activated, but that's not realistic.

Metaphorically speaking, Jeff Dion is the circus performer who spins all the plates at once - his work with the Mass Violence Survivors Fund is a side gig. In his full-time job, he's the CEO of the Zero Abuse Project, which aims to eradicate sexual abuse of minors. Jeff, himself, is a two-time victim of sexual abuse. His first experience came at the hands of an older youth, but he remained silent for fear of getting in trouble with his parents. As a 15-year-old, he was also abused by an adult in the Boy Scouts of America, an organization that was reported to have 2.1 million youth members and nearly 800,000 adult volunteers in 2019. The membership numbers, however, have dwindled over the decades, somewhat due to the abuse scandals that have continued to rock the organization. Confidence and respect for the Scouts have been decimated, and Jeff is one of the reasons.

Since the whistle blew on the organization, it's been alleged that the organization helped cover up abuse cases and failed to report the allegations to the police. Jeff spoke publicly about his scouting abuse for the first time in 2021 at the National Press Club in Washington, D.C. While wearing a sash bearing a red arrow, he detailed his 1983 camping trip to a regional scouting conference.

During that time, he was a "new and enthusiastic member of the Order of the Arrow," a secretive camping society in the scouts (hence the arrowed sash). While at Camp Shands outside Gainesville, Florida, the heavens opened and a torrential downpour soaked the area, including Jeff's tent and sleeping bag. While confiding in an adult leader there, the man offered up a spare sleeping bag and room in his tent.

"That was when he sexually abused me," Jeff told the reporters. "I didn't disclose the abuse to anyone. I was more than willing to buy into the culture of silence because I knew that speaking out could jeopardize my chances of becoming an Eagle [Scout], and that was too important."

The abuser was arrested a few years later for, not surprisingly, abusing boys in his troop, but Jeff, at this point a legal adult, still didn't speak out because he thought the man was no longer a danger to others like him.

"What I failed to realize then was that pedophiles don't retire," he said.

Jeff's press conference got national attention, and a photo of him holding up his Boy Scout Handbook was published by various media outlets. Next to him in the photo was a man named Jeff Anderson, who founded Zero Abuse Project and has probably sued the Catholic Church for child sex abuse more times than anyone in the United States.

Working hand in hand, the two Jeffs have been a thorn in the side of the church for years and have urged lawmakers to lift the statute of limitations on civil claims of sexual abuse to allow survivors more time to file claims against their abusers. In layman's terms, they've pushed for a retroactive civil window allowing old cases to come forward. The men know that it can take time (in Jeff's case, decades) to come forward finally. They've been incredibly successful, too. New York changed its law in 2019 and instituted a one-year window for adult survivors of child sexual abuse to sue an abuser or a negligent institution, no matter how long ago the abuse took place. It also allowed survivors of child sex abuse to file a civil suit until their 55th birthday, an increase from the previous age limit of 23. The state expected so many lawsuits that 45 judges were set aside to deal exclusively with these cases. The changing of the law also allowed for Jeffrey Epstein's victims to file civil lawsuits against the late multimillionaire's estate.

In Minnesota, Jeff Dion lobbied to extend the statute of limitations there, and, like New York, a window for past abuse survivors was opened — a three-year window. Minnesota was his baby, as he led the operation to change the laws so that pedophiles could be punished for decades-old acts.

The statute of limitations extensions sent shockwaves through the Boy Scouts and the Catholic Church. In Minnesota alone, Jeff Dion's legislative lobbying allowed for Jeff Anderson to file 900 child sex abuse cases in that three-year window, and about one-third of them were against the Archdiocese of Minneapolis-St. Paul. Unable to handle the lawsuits, the Archdiocese filed for bankruptcy and those cases were settled in bankruptcy for $240 million.

The Jeffs successfully changed the statute of limitations laws in Minnesota, Arizona, California, New York and New Jersey. Jeff Dion has also petitioned to have laws changed in Colorado and Pennsylvania, the latter of which is working on passing statute of limitations reform.

When Mary Jo spoke with Jeff on that airplane after the victims' conference, he was actually flying to California to represent molestation victims of the Catholic church. The following year, somewhat due to his work, California changed its law regarding the statute of limitations for child sexual abuse. Although these laws weren't explicitly aimed at the Catholic Church, the religious institution felt the effects. In California's law, a three-year "lookback window" was opened, giving victims a chance to bring civil suits against their predators and the institutions that covered for them, regardless of how long ago the crime occurred. The law also extended the civil statute of limitations to age 40 and widened the definition of childhood sexual abuse to childhood sexual assault.

"The statute of limitations hurts no one but victims, and it helps no one but perpetrators," Jeff often says.

In 2016, the Oscar-winning film *Spotlight* was released. The film chronicled an investigative news team's work to bring light to years of abuse and cover-up by the Boston Archdiocese. Jeff is his own Spotlight, but he's taken it further, given that he's been at the forefront of changing laws and paving the way for predators to pay for their crimes.

At a press conference in Pennsylvania, Jeff said, "(Pedophiles) use the statute of limitations as a shield. They know they don't have to keep victims quiet forever. They just have to keep them quiet long enough to run out the clock."

This isn't happening on Jeff Dion's watch.

Like Carroll Ellis said: "Nobody puts baby in the corner."

CHAPTER 4

Lindsay Lawler

It was supposed to be the best day of her life, and it was. But Lindsay Lawler's wedding day was also an unmitigated disaster.

For two weeks leading up to June 16, 2007, North Texas was basically underwater. The heavens had been giving the southwest region of the United States dose after dose of unrelenting precipitation. There was record flooding and rainfall all over the area. People were losing their lives, their homes, their pets and their property. Some residents needed to be rescued from floodwaters. Lakes were swollen, and rivers were beginning to overflow. There was no reprieve in sight. Flights were being diverted and canceled, and railroad tracks were buckling.

Things were so bad that President Bush declared Texas a major disaster area.

Lindsay Lawler and her fiancée Seamus Frawley wouldn't be swayed, determined to have their wedding as planned in McKinney, Texas, at the Storybook Ranch, an adorable property resembling an old Western movie set with 21 authentic buildings from the late 1800s.

The ranch, a popular wedding venue about 30 miles northeast of Dallas, sat on 80 acres with abundant trees, wildflowers, breathtaking water features and a natural creek. The believable western town always proved to be the highlight of Storybook, as it included a grand opry house, saloon, general store, jail, bank, barbershop, bell tower and chapel modeled after a turn-of-the-century church in Texas. Antique dark walnut church pews sat under the sun and faced the chapel, adorned with original stained glass from the more than 100-year-old Adolphus Hotel in Dallas. An apothecary contained original medicines from famed pharmacist and chemist Eli Lilly. The Dallas Morning News claimed that Playboy once photographed a naked woman in an upstairs red bathtub at the property's Victorian house. The magazine returned years later for a follow-up shoot. *Gunsmoke* actor Ken Curtis even filmed a movie at Storybook. (The little town within a town eventually became the victim of progress, as a developer bought the land and turned it into a master-planned community of cottage homes.)

Lindsay and Seamus had leaned into their surroundings — all the groomsmen readied themselves in the saloon and wore sheriff's badges and cowboy boots. The women all dressed in a carriage house. Lindsay, a no-nonsense gal born in Oklahoma but raised in Texas, was convinced that it wouldn't rain on her wedding day and, therefore, didn't have a backup plan. After all, heatstroke, not record rainfall, is much more of a concern in Texas summers. It should be noted that neither Seamus nor Lindsay is a meteorologist: She's a country music singer/songwriter, and he's in TV and film. His claim to fame came via working on the *Jackass* franchise, particularly the spinoff *Wildboyz*, which starred Steve-O and Chris Pontius.

The rain poured on the rehearsal dinner and didn't stop while the wedding party was getting dressed. Still, the couple was pushing forward. And it seemed they would be rewarded for their perseverance, as the severe weather stopped just minutes before Lindsay was set to be taken to the chapel in a horse-drawn buckboard and walk down the aisle in her white dress.

The problem: It was the calm before the storm.

Just 10 minutes before the couple exchanged "I do's," Lindsay boarded the horse-pulled carriage to arrive in style. The black sky was certainly ominous, but the soaked grounds added a stunning backdrop to the nuptials — the smell of wet, dark dirt hovered in the air, whipped up by howling wind.

All hell (and a horse) was about to break loose.

During her slow stroll to the ceremony, Lindsay sat in the carriage alongside her father, two flower girls and Seamus's young nephew, Nemo, who acted as the ring bearer — all of whom were internally praying the weather would hold off just long enough for the vows. Just then, the sky lit up from a lightning strike, and roaring thunder followed, causing the horse to get spooked. As it had done for weeks, the rain suddenly poured again. A total monsoon. Hoping to make the best of a bad situation, the coachman got off his seat to calm the rattled horse. That little decision, however, only added to the chaos. With nobody holding the reins, the steed jumped up instantly, his front legs suddenly parallel to the ground. Nemo, who was all of 4 years old, fell out of the carriage, landing in a pile of fresh red-hued mud, ruining his clean, pressed white shirt and black suit. He was nearly trampled.

While the coachman tended to Nemo on the soggy ground, the four-legged mammal began galloping hard and fast as Lindsay, her father and the two flower girls remained aboard. There was no driver, so the horse made all the decisions.

The terrified and drenched wedding party, all gawking at the animal anarchy, began scurrying away as the horse kicked up mud on Lindsay's dress and ran like a burglar in the night. Eventually, the horse got under control, but the downpour was already attempting to ruin the day. Nicely dressed guests all solemnly stared at Lindsay's runner, the one she was supposed to walk down before becoming a married woman, floating away in the wash. White chairs that had housed guests' rear ends just moments earlier suffered a similar fate.

"Save yourselves! Everyone take shelter!" one of the 200 wedding guests shouted, alluding to a covered area nearby.

During the retreat, elderly guests fell into muddy terrain. Lindsay and her bridesmaids, who meticulously perfected their makeup and hair in the carriage house, looked like drowned rats. Water dripped off them as if they were leaky faucets.

If this were a movie starring a comedy star, it would be funny, maybe even a rom com, but this was real life.

With the wedding not going as planned, scared guests quickly moved from a tented area to an indoor opry house, which was already set to be the location of the post-nuptial reception. There, the couple assumed people would be safe and dry.

The wedding had turned into a fiasco, but Lindsay's bridesmaids were still supporting their girl, who was devastated. With water soaking through their dresses, the bridesmaids circled the woman of the hour.

"Not one of you better tell me that this will be a good story one day. And I do not want to hear it's good luck to rain on your wedding day," Lindsay sternly said, looking every one of them in the eye.

Following the precipitation-forced audible, Lindsay and Seamus tied the knot inside the opry house to rousing applause, and the party was on… until it wasn't. Donning her mud-dotted white dress, a shattered Lindsay relaxed in a wooden chair and double-fisted glasses of champagne, something she very much earned considering the day. She looked out over the party, forcing a smile as the humidity and moisture whirled.

Watching her wedding guests make the best of a bad situation, Lindsay's mother began moving toward the bride with a look of concern.

"We have a problem," Karen Lawler informed the new bride as rain pelted the roof, sounding like marbles hitting tin cans. "The creek is flooding. If we don't get up the hill now, we'll all be stuck here tonight."

A creek, once minuscule and largely decorative, was now growing like a hosted parasite and would soon separate the wedding from civilization.

"You've got to be fucking kidding me," Lindsay responded while sitting on the floor, arms and legs crossed, insinuating she wasn't going anywhere. With mascara tears running down her face and her hair extensions barely hanging on, she staunchly pouted, "I'm not leaving!"

There hadn't even been time for pictures of the bride and groom around the seven-tiered wedding cake.

Despite the bride's insistence, there was no choice. They had to get the hell out of Dodge — and quickly! Mother Nature was being a real nasty bitch.

With the defeated wedding coordinator hunched over, crying in a corner of the room and offering absolutely zero help, the *Jackass* crew, several of whom were wedding guests, jumped into work mode. To them, this was like producing and directing a movie. A horror movie, maybe, but a movie.

Jeff Tremaine, who co-created *Jackass*, and Trip Taylor, a producer of the MTV franchise, grabbed walkie-talkies and began running the show.

"All hands on deck," Jeff and Trip announced as they began conducting the hasty evacuation.

Guests were loaded into SUVs, trucks, and anything with off-road capability, which there is no shortage of in the Lone Star State. Flowers, booze, decor and anything that wasn't nailed down were tossed into vehicles at the *Jackass* guys' orders. The wedding cake was placed in the back of a Land Rover (Jeff and Trip hovered over the tall, sweet confection to minimize rain damage.) Dumbfounded over what was happening, the new bride and groom sat in the middle row of the four-wheel drive vehicle as it sped off to outrun the storm.

Like a wave in the ocean, water deluged the hood of the Land Rover as it plowed through the rapid, vicious, and rising creek that threatened to strand the wedding party. It was a rough ride!

"It looked like a Land Rover commercial," Lindsay later quipped.

The caravan of vehicles eventually found higher ground and descended on an empty barn on top of a hill. With Jeff and Trip producing their latest masterpiece — albeit unaccredited on IMDB — guests braved the elements and assisted in moving the booze, moving food and carrying flowers. The DJ, thankfully a friend, moved his equipment four times.

The high-sitting barn was basic, but also the best-case scenario. After all, it was covered, dry and had functioning lights and electrical outlets. In the blink of an eye and under the direction of well-seasoned TV and movie producers, tables were set up, music was starting to pump out of speakers and smiles started forming on faces.

Finally, there was normalcy and tranquility for the first time in several hours.

The tide was turning on an unforgettable-for-all-the-wrong-reasons day. Honestly, the makeshift reception looked stunning, especially when considering everything was done on the fly. This wasn't how Lindsay had envisioned beginning her married life, but it was good in a pinch.

As soon as the deejay dropped beats, guests scurried to the dance floor like vultures on roadkill. It seemed everyone needed to let off some steam, and did they ever.

Needless to say, it was the most memorable wedding any of the guests had ever experienced. The best sign of a good time? They ran out of vodka... twice.

The wedding's craziness even brought people closer, including Lindsay and Seamus's parents, who'd only ever met that day - a true silver lining stemming directly from the pandemonium that had taken place.

"We always joke that our wedding was like *Meet The Fockers* from the side of our parents," Lindsay says, referring to the Ben Stiller and Robert DeNiro classic, "but they got along splendidly, so we were thrilled."

The bride and groom's parents couldn't be more different, particularly from the male side. Lindsay's father, an insurance attorney, is the absolute cliche of a staunch Texas conservative (although he did some modeling and played in a college band called The Geese). Seamus' father is a poet and painter with a thick Boston accent, who somewhat jokingly asked in the days leading up to the wedding, "At what point can I start making jokes about George Bush?" to which the bride and groom in unison announced, "NEVER!"

With everything happening at the wedding, guests from all regions, religions and walks of life were forced to join the same team. The chaos was unifying.

Despite her earlier declaration to her bridesmaids, the catastrophe of that Texas afternoon did make for a good story, and Lindsay eventually recorded a song called "Rain on My Wedding Day," documenting the fiasco. She sings: "Don't tell me it'll all be okay, 'cause all I dreamed of has all washed away. I've been planning this since I was eight. I don't wanna hear it's good luck to rain on my wedding day."

All these years later, Lindsay and Seamus remain happily married and have settled into a much less stormy life. In 2018, following two failed adoptions, they formally adopted their daughter Freya June, who was born in Arkansas and of Marshallese descent. Lindsay also hosts a radio show on SiriusXM for the trucking industry, is followed on Twitter by Barack Obama, and has performed at the Capitol in D.C. for the lighting of the Christmas Tree, Arlington Cemetery, and CMA Fest, the world's most preeminent country music festival.

Seamus, meanwhile, is dotting father and one of the more renowned sound mixers in entertainment, continuing to work on *Jackass* specials and movies. Similarly, he was part of the production team for Dolly Parton's 2023 special, *From Rhinestones to Rock & Roll,* and has worked over 100 TV shows with noted biologist and wildlife conservationist Jeff Cornwin.

Maybe the rain on their wedding day was good luck after all.

September 2023

On a picture-perfect June day, Lindsay Lawler is walking down a scenic, tree-lined road near her home in Franklin, Tenn., a booming and affluent suburb of Nashville home to a glut of music stars. Those who lived there or still live there include Tim McGraw and Faith Hill, Kathie Lee Gifford, Justin Timberlake, Keith Urban and Nicole Kidman and Carrie Underwood. Miley Cyrus has a 33-acre farm in Franklin, and Oprah once had a property there. The list of notable tenants goes on and on.

Today, the newest members of the Franklin community are De and Karen Lawler, Lindsay's parents, having just relocated from Dallas.

Flanked by her mom and dad during this serene stroll, the trio is making small talk and discussing Freya June's latest milestones. Suddenly, the unmistakable sound of a guitar infiltrates the air, and they soon see why when stumbling upon a 16-year-old girl riffing on her six-string. Like Wayne and Karen, the girl is new to the area.

"You sound great," Lindsay tells her new, much younger neighbor, who is already rather accomplished on the guitar.

"We just moved here," the teen offers. "My family all came out here to chase my dream, and hopefully, you'll hear my music on the radio."

Looking at her parents, Lindsay couldn't help herself.

"Her whole family gave up their lives to move here for her career," she said half-jokingly.

Lindsay's music career wasn't always something that her parents understood. They always supported her, mind you, but also probably thought of it more as her hobby - a cool hobby — but still a hobby. Sure, she was the lead singer of a band in college, but that would be a fad, her parents assumed.

Factor 9, a rock band, came into Lindsay's life in the most unconventional way: a Post-It Note.

Musical as a child, Lindsay, like so many others, started out by singing in church. She soon upgraded to country bars, where she learned up close the rough-and-tumble grind of honky tonk singers — she also learned a few curse words too. Unable and unwilling to move on from her church choir beginnings, Lindsay soon became the song leader of her sorority, Kappa Alpha Theta. One day, while aimlessly strolling around Oklahoma University in her "sorority-issued" black pants, she came upon a yellow note stuck to an overgrown tree.

"Rock Band Looking For Lead Singer." The note had a contact number, which Lindsay decided to call.

Less than a week later, she pulled up to an off-campus home. The garage was open, and there stood three guys. One man was holding a guitar, another a bass, and one sat behind a drum kit.

"I'm Lindsay."

"Let's see what you can do," one of the men, apparently the band leader, said after initial introductions. He suggested they start with Led Zeppelin's "Dazed and Confused," a 1969 song Lindsay had never heard. Still, she learned it on the fly in just a few minutes.

"Ok, I think I'm good to go."

Lindsay hadn't exactly been a rock singer, but she had the voice and vocal range for it. During this otherwise typical garage jam session, she didn't hold back, first mastering that Robert Plant and Jimmy Page classic and then moving on to a few more cover songs from the '70s and '80s.

"Ok," the band leader said, "I think I've heard enough."

Lindsay smirked and giggled to herself but said nothing.

"When can you start?"

Without missing a beat, she confidently asserted, "I think we just did."

From that moment, she fronted Factor 9, and they recorded music and toured much of the Southwest. Still, Factor 9 wasn't her endgame, and she knew it, but that stint helped her break out of her conservative mentality. She realized that a whole world existed, full of interesting people — a world of broken and fun people, of thoughtful and provocative people, of simple-minded and philosophical people. She was hooked on the tapestry of it all. She went into the band as a sheltered and curious girl who always did right and stayed in her lane, but she emerged as a take-no-prisoners extrovert who happily took chances. She embraced the beautiful weirdness of the world before her.

After graduating from Oklahoma University in three years with a degree in journalism, it wasn't clear what Lindsay would do next. The roller coaster of parental emotions continued. Naturally, they were on a high knowing their daughter graduated early, but Lindsay threw them for a loop and took a hard left turn when deciding to live with her grandparents and continue pursuing music with her college band. To make ends meet, she worked for an office supply company not unlike the one portrayed in *The Office,* but less funny and with no one as handsome as John Krasinski.

Her parents always assumed radio communication would be Lindsay's life's work, knowing full well she wouldn't follow the path of her older sister, Lisken, who has worked in the corporate offices of Pizza Hut and GameStop. But Lindsay was determined to be a star, much like her high school classmate and former chorus line partner Jessica Simpson (yes, that Jessica Simpson).

2002

Following a quick stint in Dallas working with nationally syndicated radio host Kidd Kraddick, Lindsay, a fresh college graduate, took her talents to Los Angeles in 2002, where she joined and fronted the metal-adjacent Ciattic, a band that took inspiration from Motley Crue, Twisted Sister, Poison, Dokken and just about every other hair group of the same ilk. Lindsay was only recently removed from college, but her three bandmates, who'd been together since the 80s, were all 20 years her senior and still held tight to their mullets and belief that Aqua-Net was the world's only hairspray. MTV's "Headbanger's Ball," a show that celebrated hard rock, was a religion to them. With Ciattic, Lindsay was a familiar face on the Sunset Strip, having performed at Whisky-A-Go-Go, Viper Room and The Roxy, all legendary places in their own right, and her powerful vocals and onstage charisma gave life to the songs. Ciattic even recorded a full-length album and toured. Since Lindsay's style steered more toward boho-chic, the guitar player's wife made her clothes so she'd have fashion harmony with the aging rockers of Ciattic.

"It was a bizarre time in my life," Lindsay laughs, admitting that she never really understood the metal music she was singing.

Although Lindsay now saw that stint as semi-comical, her friends saw it differently. Laura Tremaine, Lindsay's college roommate and sorority sister in Kappa Alpha Theta at Oklahoma University in the late 90s, was shocked after attending a Ciattic show in L.A.'s South Bay. Watching

Lindsay shred through lyrics amid screeching electric guitars was not what Laura was used to, but it somehow fit.

"It was fun to watch, and she was good at it, but it didn't really square with who she is as a human," Laura said. "Maybe that's why it surprised me because she's not hard-etched at all."

Despite being roommates and sharing similar geographical upbringings, Lindsay and Laura's personalities differ somewhat. Lindsay is more of an extrovert and social butterfly, whereas Laura is more introverted and a total bookworm. She openly calls herself a "nerd."

The women complemented each other nicely. Lindsay broke Laura out of her shell, whereas Laura kept Lindsay a little more grounded and tethered to her roots.

One day in college, after hearing about the formation of Lindsay's college band, Factor 9, Laura decided to see her friend on stage at an area called Campus Corner, a college-oriented district known for its bar and diverse retail shops. Laura had watched Lindsay perform before, but something about this show stood out.

"I think it was the first time I realized how serious she was about it, and I knew this is what she was meant to do," Laura said. "I remember thinking not only is it brave for her to get up on a stage, but it felt really brave that she was busting out these sort of norms of the world that we lived in at the time."

On stage, Lindsay belted out original material and cover songs. She was engaging and talented. You wanted to be her.

"Naked ambition of that type of performance was not normal," Laura said, noting that few women were really making it as a true frontwoman of a band at the time.

Make no mistake about it: Lindsay was giving it her all to become a successful singer. She was grinding away in college, and then she was grinding away in Los Angeles, where she again lived with Laura, who had set up roots on the West Coast a year prior.

It soon became apparent that Lindsay wasn't becoming the star she thought, but Los Angeles would prove to be life-changing, especially after Lindsay accompanied Laura, a production assistant, to a wrap party for a TV show called *Wildboyz*, a Jackass spinoff involving animals and wildlife. There, she noticed this man from across the room, and he noticed her. Laura already knew the man because they worked together and were friends. His name was Seamus.

"Seamus, this is my friend Lindsay," Laura said in an introduction, hardly thinking she was playing matchmaker. "Lindsay, this is Seamus. We worked together on the show. I love Seamus."

Seamus and Lindsay exchanged hellos and went their separate ways, but they found each other at the bar again later and started talking.

Typically, getting Lindsay out of social environments is tough because she is hardwired to speak to everyone. That night, her focus was set on this man, Seamus, and the two actually walked out holding hands.

"Are you girls coming to the after party?" he asked Lindsay and Laura, to which they declined. Lindsay never gave Seamus her phone number; social media was in its infancy and hardly a way to contact people. Still, she knew in her heart that she'd somehow see him again.

A few weeks later, Lindsay went to a nondescript office building in Los Angeles to pick up Laura before seeing a friend's play. While waiting for her roommate near the printer at the post-production office, Seamus suddenly appeared in the room. He had to retrieve something he had printed. Clearly, this document was important and dealt with filming the next *Jackass* installment. At least, that's what Lindsay thought.

"I didn't have anything to print," he later confessed. "I just printed the homepage of AOL so I could go talk to her."

He wasn't ready to give up on that conversation they'd started at the wrap party.

Seamus was hardly the kind of guy Lindsay thought she'd ever be with. In high school, she was the head cheerleader and dated the captain of the football team. She got good grades and had an impeccable attendance record. Despite her run as frontwoman of a metal band, she was still sort of that goodie-two-shoes girl. Seamus was a surfer and skateboarder. In high school, sometimes he showed up for class, and sometimes the ocean's waves were too good to pass up. In her eyes, Seamus is a little bit of a bad boy, but he's also driven to be successful in everything, be it work, in his marriage or as a father. Lindsay liked Seamus for who he was, but she also subconsciously tried to find the guy who, on paper, her family would've never picked. He fit the bill perfectly, but he was also a good man. He checked all the boxes.

The evening Lindsay met Seamus, he was discussing politics with Laura at that wrap party. They were pretty much on opposite sides of the aisle, but both completely respected the other's views, a rather uncommon trait in L.A. The conversation was thoughtful and intellectual. If Lindsay had met Seamus in high school, she would have been scared of someone who was more misfit than Mr. Football.

"He's always been that juxtaposition of all these worlds," Lindsay says. "He's the perfect balance of excitement and intrigue and socially unacceptable. I wouldn't know how to talk to someone like that in high school."

Lindsay found everything she wanted in her personal life in Los Angeles, and she couldn't say "yes" fast enough when Seamus proposed. Yes, L.A. had been a dream for her personal life, but her career was at a stalemate a bit, largely because she saw her future about 2,000 miles away in Nashville. Seamus, though, had a lot of work in Los Angeles, so the idea of moving to the South seemed remote. Romancing the idea of Tennessee life in her mind, she delicately expressed her desire to move to Music City, USA, but never forced it on him. She was certain that it would have to be at Seamus' suggestion if they were ever to move to Nashville because she didn't want to be to blame if it didn't work out.

At the time, little was happening in Nashville in terms of film production, certainly not compared to L.A. There was a legitimate chance that Seamus might have to start over from scratch if they moved. However, he also wholeheartedly believed in his partner's dream and was willing to sacrifice his career for hers.

Happy wife, happy life.

"If you think we should move to Nashville, let's go," a text message from her soon-to-be husband flashed across Lindsay's cell phone on a Tuesday. Wasting no time, they moved that Friday. Laura was devastated. In the blink of an eye, she lost two friends to Middle America.

September 2007

In Nashville, the couple settled into their routines and new Southern lives, which is precisely where Lindsay felt most at home. Granted, they had their struggles and wondered if they'd made the biggest mistake of their lives moving to a new city as newlyweds with no jobs, friends or a place to live. Something felt right, though. Back to her roots, Lindsay was able to shake off that odd stint as the lead singer of a metal band and began booking music gigs at Tootsie's Orchid Lounge, arguably the most legendary honky tonk in Nashville.

Surrounded by bars as far as the eye can see, Tootsie's stands out in the lower Broadway area of Nashville due to its rich purple facade. Back in 1960, Hattie Louise "Tootsie" Bess purchased a bar called Mom's in the lower Broadway area of Nashville. Wanting to give the building a bit of a facelift, she hired a local painter but didn't give him much direction. One day, she walked in and found the walls painted orchid purple. Because of the paint job, Mom's was renamed Tootsie's Orchid Lounge.

Located just behind the Ryman Auditorium, which housed the Grand Ole Opry from 1943 to 1974, Tootsie's quickly became a hangout for established country music stars. Dolly Parton, Kris Kristofferson, Charlie Pride, Waylon Jennings, Patsy Cline and more were seen hanging out there in the early days. It's still quite common to see celebrities from all walks of life there. The Tootsies stages — of which there are three — have become proving grounds for aspiring artists, too. Taylor Swift, Keith Urban and Toby Keith have all played there. The bar even alleges that Willie Nelson got his first songwriting job after singing at Tootsie's. Pink played a surprise show there in 2019 after a sold-out concert at the nearby Bridgestone Arena, and the Country Music Hall of Fame and Museum honored the honky tonk with a photo exhibit in 2011.

Lindsay played the stage at Tootsie's for several years, the same stages graced by those aforementioned country music icons, but it wasn't always smooth sailing. In those early Tootsie's days, Lindsay was terrified on stage. She didn't play guitar or bass or anything. Instead, her voice was her instrument, but she didn't know if the crowd or management would accept her or pay any attention to the vocals. When customers started returning to see her on stage, she knew something was working. When Kenny Chesney and The Wailers joined her on stage, she knew something was working. When Kid Rock joined her on stage, she knew something was working.

"You sing like an angel," the rocker shouted to Lindsay before joining her for a rendition of his song "Cowboy."

John Ratliff, Lindsay's friend and colleague, recalled the first time seeing her perform in Nashville, which occurred four hours after they met at The Nashville Music Loft, a pristine 2,740 square foot condo that Lindsay has long managed and John would eventually purchase (she still manages the condo). When John met Lindsay, she was kind and humble. Soft-spoken, actually.

"I'm playing tonight on Broadway at Whiskey Bent. You should come," she told John, referring to one of the many honky-tonks in Nashville's top tourist region.

Maybe curiosity got the best of him because he wasn't convinced this diminutive woman could hold an audience. He thought it could be a trainwreck, and those can be fun to watch.

That evening, John bellied up to the Whiskey Bent bar as his feet lightly stuck to the beer-saturated wooden floor. The crowd was spirited and rowdy, as it usually was. He watched as Lindsay and her band set up and truly hoped she would at least not embarrass herself. He set a low bar for her, basing it strictly on their incredibly brief dealing at the loft.

As soon as Lindsay opened her mouth, his eyes and ears got way more than he bargained for.

"It was the classic Jekyll and Hyde situation," he remembered. "She's five-foot-whatever tall, but has a massive stage presence."

At many Nashville honky tonks, the music can be comparable to wallpaper and sometimes not noticeable. Guests are typically more interested in the drinks and vibe, which is why barhopping is the norm. Broadway performers, and there are plenty of them, can blend into the bar easily and quickly. Lindsay, though, was commanding the room, which was full of drunks, college kids and bachelorette parties, many of whom sucked their drinks through penis-shaped straws.

John was engrossed and couldn't look away, nor could the rest of the bar. He was happily wrong about Lindsay. He was watching this woman work in her genius.

"Who was that woman I met at the loft a few hours ago?" he wondered, realizing he didn't give her nearly enough credit.

Over the years, the two developed a friendship, and John, a serial entrepreneur, has seen her many times, including at the musical institution that is Tootsie's.

"I love sitting back and watching people experience Lindsay on stage for the first time," he said.

One day, while taking a break from the purple-toned walls of Tootsie's, Lindsay booked a gig in Dallas to perform at an event called the Great American Trucking Show, something that would alter her path. At the show, she heard about the Highway Angel program, a non-profit organization that recognizes truck drivers for kindness, good deeds and heroic acts while on the road. With that, Lindsay found her next calling. It was that quick. She was floored by the generosity of the truckers and loved everything she was being shown and told. In her epiphany, she realized she wanted to help truckers and bring attention to their lives, their plights and everything in between.

"I realized that I was equally excited to be at dinner with the billionaire truck company owner or the guy with one truck that's just making his living driving home," she said.

Before long, she wrote and recorded the song "Highway Angel", which became an anthem for the eponymous program and served as the organization's ambassador and spokesperson. She wrote another song for female truck drivers, "For the Long Haul," in which she sings: "Nobody said it would be easy running against the wind." The songs have depth and meaning and don't grasp the low-hanging fruit and stereotypes.

While she's never had a record deal — nor has she really tried to score one — the trucking industry became her niche and took her to places she never thought she'd go, which included performing in the Capitol for the lighting of the National Christmas Tree and at Arlington National Ceremony, the latter of which came via her work with Wreaths Across America, an organization that lays wreaths delivered by truckers at military gravesites.

Her love of all things 18 wheels soon caught the attention of legendary trucking radio host Dave Nemo and SiriusXM's Road Dog Trucking channel, which promotes itself as a 24-hour channel devoted to the industry. As co-host of The Weekend 34, Lindsay provides four hours of entertainment via music or interviews with songwriters, authors or actors. Truckers are a loyal, dedicated, and captivated audience, primarily because they have ample time to listen to the radio, and her name is prominent within that community.

The Weekend 34, whose name comes from the 34-hour break truckers are mandated to take, scored a significant moment when famed astrophysicist and writer Neil deGrasse Tyson stopped by in 2023.

"I had never talked to somebody like that. I'm like, 'What am I going to talk to an astrophysicist about?'" she said. "When I heard we were going to have him on, I went into full panic mode."

For all the sweating and second-guessing, things couldn't have gone better. Neil was slated for 20 minutes on the show, but he ended up staying for an hour.

"This is such a fun interview! You guys really know your stuff and asked such different, insightful questions," he told Lindsay off-air when she asked if he'd be up for staying on air longer.

Her radio prowess isn't by accident. She learned under the aforementioned Kraddick and was an on-air producer at Star 98.7 in Los Angeles, where Ryan Seacrest was the host. It was there, in the City of Angels, that Lindsay met her soon-to-be lifelong friend Tiffany Darwish.

Tiffany, an L.A. native, knew the music scene from all avenues and had been a part of it since she was a teen. Tiffany, known mononymously by only her first name, burst onto the scene in 1987 when she recorded her pop-heavy cover of Tommy James and the Shondells song "I Think We're Alone Now," which spent two weeks at No. 1.

Tiffany adored country music in her prepubescent years and often performed covers of Tanya Tucker, Tammy Wynette and Emmylou Harris at local fairs and school assemblies. After hearing Stevie Nicks for the first time, she was utterly enthralled. She began meshing country, rock and pop and signed a record deal with MCA. While her debut single flopped, she struck gold—platinum, actually — with her rendition of "I Think We're Alone Now." Her follow-up single, "Could've Been," while lesser known than its predecessor, also hit No. 1 on the Billboard charts.

Tiffany's mainstream music success was well behind her when Lindsay entered her life, but the two became fast friends after realizing their similarities.

"She's hippy-dippy do. I'm hippy-dippy do," Tiffany says of their shared personalities. "We both like a cocktail here and there. We both believed in holistic medicine. We have the L.A. connection. We're both performers."

When Tiffany moved to Nashville over a decade ago, one of her first calls was to Lindsay.

"Hey, Miss Radio," Tiffany said, using her nickname for her friend, "I want to hit the ground running. Give me the lay of the land."

Tiffany had spent significant time in Nashville, even doing mall tours there decades prior, but she trusted Lindsay to be her on-the-ground insider.

The teen sensation found her footing with Lindsay's guidance and started reverting to her roots, releasing and writing a country album called Rose Tattoo. It was a full-circle moment. Although Tiffany never wanted to shed her pop past completely, country was in her soul.

The album, Rose Tattoo, featured eight tracks, including "Crazy Girls," which was written with Lindsay, who also dueted on the song. This, of course, was not the Tiffany of old — this wasn't the one who broke her squeaky-clean image in posing for Playboy in 2003, which she has no regrets about; this wasn't the Tiffany who moved into her grandmother's home after attempting to become an emancipated minor. This Tiffany, well into her 30s at that point, realized that her friendships, especially the one shared with Lindsay, were unbreakable.

Frankly, Lindsay was different, too. When Tiffany first met Lindsay, "Miss Radio" whimsically toiled around L.A., attending parties and singing metal music. When the women had more thoughtful conversations, and there were many, they had deep chats about motherhood, especially given that Tiffany had welcomed a son as a 21-year-old. Lindsay hadn't given children much thought in her younger years, but she confided in Tiffany about her desire to be a mother as times changed. In Nashville, Tiffany was able to see "Miss Radio" as a mother.

The Frothy Monkey is a Tennessee success story. The all-day cafe opened in a 1,200-square-foot bungalow in Nashville's trendy 12 South area and quickly expanded to nine locations, seven of which are in the Volunteer State. Guests at the coffeehouse can get a caffeine fix, snack from its impressive menu of entrees, sandwiches, salads or baked goods, or imbibe on beer and wine. It was here, at the Downtown Franklin location, that Tiffany met Freya June, who was then just four months old.

Amid hot lattes, the "Crazy Girls" songwriters talked shop and watched young Freya look curiously at the ceiling lights. Although sleep-deprived and terribly exhausted like all new parents, Lindsay was beaming. The era of Lindsay and Tiffany's six-hour lunches and drink-a-thons was over. Coffee, much needed in Lindsay's case, now replaced tequila.

Tiffany was years removed from having an infant but could still relate to her friends' ethos.

"Is she sleeping through the night? Are YOU sleeping through the night?"

"No to both."

There were questions about tummy time, formulas, SIDS and milestones. Boy, oh boy, had their conversations shifted!

That day, however, is unforgettable to Tiffany. It was the first time she saw Lindsay not just as a friend and a singer/songwriter, but as a caregiver. A photo from The Frothy Monkey visit sits in Tiffany's home. In it, she's holding little Freya while Lindsay stands next to her. Several years later, Aunt Tiffany gave Freya a gift: a My Little Pony toy, which Freya still has.

"Freya," Tiffany said while visiting her friend's Franklin home, "this is for you. You need some 80s in your life. It's not normal if you don't."

October 2017

It was a few days into October and Lindsay Lawler was crying at her home on the outskirts of Nashville. The entire country was still shaken and in deep reflection after a gunman opened fire on a concert crowd in Las Vegas on Oct. 1. In some ways, Nashville was every bit as broken as Las Vegas following the shooting because of the country music connection. Like so many people, Lindsay was consumed with not just the story, as sensational as it was, but also the 58 people who'd lost their lives. She read about Jordan McIldoon, who was five days shy of his 24th birthday; she heard about Jordyn Rivera, a lovable college student who died in her mother's arms; she learned of Michelle Vo, a new country fan who attended the show solo. While there, she struck up a friendship with Kody Robertson. After she was shot, Kody tried to save Michelle, essentially a total stranger, and was the one who informed her family of her passing.

The Vo family calls Kody their "guardian angel" to his day. Naturally, Lindsay also read about Kurt.

"He was a trucker," Lindsay told nobody in particular after reading about Kurt von Tillow.

Following a moment of reflection, the wheels in her head started turning as she found herself logging onto Facebook and searching for family members. She didn't realize that the von Tillow family was being bombarded by the media, well-wishers and, yes, vultures looking to capitalize on the situation.

In a message to Dee Ann Hyatt, Kurt's sister, Lindsay explained who she was and detailed her connection to the trucking industry. As a spokesperson for Highway Angel, she was always seeking out inspirational stories to bring attention to, and she felt that Kurt should be honored posthumously for his contributions to trucking.

Every year, Highway Angel honors truckers for various things, whether saving a life, changing a stranger's tire or even delivering a baby. Kurt needed his moment among his peers at a trucking convention, Lindsay felt. In theory, this should have been a no-brainer for Mary Jo and Kurt's siblings, but their family didn't know who to trust in the immediate fallout of the shooting. Lindsay, they thought, could be a scam artist. Lord knows there was no shortage of them rearing their heads.

Fortunately, Mary Jo and a few family members would be in Nashville in November for the Country Music Awards, which also honored Kurt and the 58 victims, so they decided to meet with Lindsay at the Thompson Hotel.

"We all had their guards up," Mary Jo recalled, "but we were willing to listen to her."

While peering down at the Nashville skyline, they listened to Lindsay eloquently speak about her life, her marriage, her career and her connection to trucking. The von Tillows all immediately felt at ease and knew this woman was trying to do right by Kurt. During a moment of casual chatting, Mary

Jo offhandedly said, "Kurt's birthday is coming up, so that's going to be a really tough day."

"I don't know why, but I have this feeling that Kurt and I have the same birthday," Lindsay uttered. "Is his birthday December 4?"

To say they were shocked was an understatement, and the entire table burst into tears while confirming the hunch.

Lindsay was also putting on a brave face throughout the week. Just one day before landing in Nashville, Seamus' brother Ethan passed away unexpectedly in Massachusetts, and he naturally flew to the East Coast immediately. Lindsay, however, was committed to her promise to honor Mary Jo's late husband.

Just over a week later, with now two families grieving, Lindsay stepped on stage at the National Association of Small Trucking Companies annual convention at downtown Nashville's Sheraton Hotel and spoke of Kurt's life and passion for all things trucking.

Conventions are popular for all industries, and it's commonplace to have an annual theme. The NASTC's theme that year was "Leading At Every Turn," a befitting slogan for Kurt, as he was the family leader and ahead of the times with his music and sports preferences. The Dave Nemo Show, on which Lindsay appears, was broadcast live from the convention.

Sitting in the convention space before a round, white linen-covered table, the von Tillow team clutched onto a photo of Kurt and listened as a few local singers performed pensive songs. They all forced smiles through the melancholy of the moment. After gathering themselves, Lindsay presented them with the Highway Angel award, which was accepted on Kurt's behalf.

"The feeling was bittersweet, but seeing hundreds of Kurt's peers giving him a standing ovation was heartwarming," Mary Jo said.

The family was still very much raw from the shooting, but Nashville gave them the hug they needed.

Every year on Oct. 1, Las Vegas hosts a sunrise remembrance ceremony to honor the victims of the mass shooting. It's usually attended by local dignitaries like the Nevada Governor, the Clark County Sheriff and the Las Vegas Mayor. Surviving family members are given the opportunity to speak, too. In 2021, Dee Ann alluded to Kurt's award, stating that fellow truckers and Lindsay's generosity were "the beginning of some really, really deep healing for our family."

One day after Kurt's posthumous award, Lindsay boarded a plane and flew to Massachusetts to be with her husband.

To no surprise, Lindsay has become a very close friend of the von Tillow family since that day, even traveling to Lake Tahoe to sing a cappella on a boat while Kurt's ashes were scattered there.

She's not blood, but she's family to the von Tillows.

2019

She was 30,000 feet in the air when she had her spiritual awakening.

Just a few days earlier, Lindsay Lawler had been attending the funeral of a trucking industry friend when a man whom she knew sexually assaulted her. In real time, the singer was shocked and almost frozen. She never thought this executive, whom she refuses to name, was capable of something so heinous. Of course, she never thought she'd be the victim of unwanted advances, either. Truckers get bad raps — much of it unwarranted — but nobody who ever sat behind a steering wheel for a living ever made her feel as uncomfortable as this man who sits behind a big oak desk.

With her headphones in her ears and tuning out the noise of the Southwest airplane's roaring engines, Lindsay listened to a podcast featuring shaman and author Durek Verrett. Suddenly, she lost it. She tried to keep her emotions inward and not call attention to herself, but she also needed to let them out and begin to process what had happened.

"I suddenly saw everything differently. I didn't think anything in the world would ever be the same," she says while reflecting on her in-air thought mentality. "The event," as she calls it, was a wake-up call.

But, despite her entire worldview shifting instantly, Lindsay tried to settle back into normalcy after returning home. She still hadn't fully come to terms with what happened, and her sleep pattern changed. She was often restless and would wake up in the middle of the night with memories of that fateful 2019 encounter.

Lindsay knew what had happened that day. She knew her abuser, as do so many women in similar situations, but she didn't know how to move forward. She certainly wasn't ready to broadcast her experience and open herself up to the judgment of strangers. Still, she needed to talk about it and clear the air. Lindsay was aware that therapy had worked for other people in the past, but was unsure if it would work for her. Then again, what did she have to lose?

Following painstaking research, Lindsay found an Idaho-based therapist with whom she quickly connected. The woman coupled spirituality and empowerment with talk therapy. During their therapy sessions, which happened on the phone, Lindsay began to believe that the assault was not her fault. This fact was drilled into her head over and over and over again. In time, not immediately, Lindsay began to believe it.

Despite "the event," Lindsay wasn't seeking retribution but didn't want to pretend it didn't happen. A money grab would have been easy, but it wasn't for her. Likewise, lawsuits weren't appealing, as she didn't want to drag her family through the mud. She also didn't want to drag her abuser's family through the mud since they had nothing to do with the man's actions.

One man committed one act. To her.

For the better part of three years, Lindsay assumed she'd do nothing about the assault and wondered if it was best to bury it deep down. Statistics show that most women involved in similar situations also do nothing, which is part of the problem.

"I didn't want to be told what to do," she said. "People would say, 'You have a responsibility.' No, what happens to other people isn't my responsibility."

Lindsay had her own life to attend to, whether it be her marriage, her child or her career. Although coming clean about her assault might be beneficial to others, it wasn't something she put a deadline on. She needed to be selfish and discover her own healing journey before even attempting to help others down the road.

In 2021, after years of keeping her assault largely quiet, Lindsay began realizing she had a platform and could address "the event" in the best way she knew how: her music and her songwriting. To do that, though, she needed to let a few people in on her secret, and it would start with fellow singer/songwriter and close friend Chris Roberts, with whom she was attending a songwriter's retreat in Key West, Florida (He was also on hand to perform when Kurt was given the Highway Angel Award in 2017.)

Having known each other since 2007, Chris and Lindsay met at a Universal Music Party in Nashville, a party that Lindsay crashed. At the time, Chris had been signed by Decca Records, which was once Bing Crosby's label. White Christmas, which Bing first recorded in 1942, is still the record label's best-selling song. Chris is no slouch, either. His songs have been used for a myriad of commercials and films. He was nominated for a Grammy for his work with H.E.R. and has performed on Broadway in New York. He's written songs for too many country artists to count and is also a well-known performer in the bluegrass world. Over the years, he's become Lindsay's trusted songwriting partner and has accompanied her to many gigs, including the ones in the Capitol building and Arlington National Cemetery. He also helped co-write "Crazy Girls," the song Lindsay and Tiffany sang together (he co-wrote several others on Tiffany's Rose Tattoo album, too).

Lindsay and Chris traveled the country so much that they developed travel monikers — no longer known by their birth names, but rather as Helena and Gordon. The "supergroup" that was Helena and Gordon had superpowers, although most of them involved charming flight attendants for free cocktails.

However, that day at the Florida songwriter's retreat had a vastly different tone than the typical Helena and Gordon adventures.

"I have an idea for a song tomorrow, but I need you to make me write it," Lindsay told Chris at dinner without any other details. Chris, though, is very pliable and can adapt to all musical genres, so she knew he could handle the potential song's sensitive nature.

The following morning, Chris met a solemn-faced Lindsay in a plain, vanilla conference room and gifted her a cup of coffee.

"What do you want to write about today?" he asked, sensing her heavy heart.

"Well," she said while getting her caffeine fix, "it's not a happy song."

"Tell me."

"Follow me."

After leading Chris and his guitar down to the adjacent beach, Lindsay slipped off her flip-flops, sunk her toes in the dry, grainy sand, stared west out into the deep, blue Gulf of Mexico and took a deep breath. He adjusted his baseball cap as a light breeze passed by. For the next hour, she told Chris everything, often crying and wiping tears from her face. The skies were a light teal that day, and the water was bright and cyan, but Lindsay felt even bluer. Chris, meanwhile, listened intently and lightly strummed his guitar, rarely speaking. His heart broke for his friend.

This was a far different Lindsay—or Helena, for that matter—than he was used to. On this day, Lindsay wasn't the gregarious, joyful artist who self-released two, soon to be three, albums and way more singles.

Wearing a beach-appropriate white coverup, she spilled her guts out, and before they knew it, the duo had a song — one that Lindsay never intended to release. This was more a song for her, for her healing. Nothing more. But something in Lindsay's soul nagged to release the song.

In April 2022, in conjunction with Sexual Assault Awareness Month, "I'm Okay" was released.

"If this body could talk would you want to hear what it's saying, see the toll it's taken?" she says in the lyrics. An accompanying music video shows Lindsay singing the song before a group of people holding candles. Her eyes look misty as she belts the song in her signature tone. A single tear runs down her face, and she makes no effort to hide it or wipe it away.

Lindsay's incident caught the attention of a People magazine writer, who penned a 2022 story about the singer entitled "Reclaiming Her Power."

The song, one never intended to be released for public consumption, had an immediate impact. Messages of hope and thankfulness poured into Lindsay's inbox and social media. It was heartwarming. Lindsay felt she made a difference and let others know they weren't alone. To that end, it was also discouraging to read so many messages from women who confided that they, too, were victims of similar situations. She also received messages from those who were involved in even more violent encounters.

While Lindsay is "okay," none of these assaults are okay.

"Ultimately, I felt that this was right," she says now. "If it helped one person outside of me, then there you go."

CHAPTER 5

Dion Green

Dion Green was 25 years old when his choices caught up with him. For years, he'd been one of the preeminent drug dealers in Ohio, often working with Mexican drug cartels to put cocaine into the area.

"I was no petty drug dealer," he flatly says now.

Although he wasn't a drug user — the best dealers seldom are — Dion was skilled at being a narcotics carrier, and he moved up the ranks of the crooked craft. Make no mistake about it: Dion was both street-smart and book smart. Although he was raised under trying circumstances — his mother basically raised him as his father was dealing with his demons — Dion threw himself into his education. He earned an MBA in Business Administration from Keller's Graduate School and a Bachelor of Science in Business Administration from DeVry University.

In his 20s, a 9-to-5 wasn't the route for him, so he turned to more unsavory employment. Drug running was more than paying the bills, and Dion soon owned businesses and houses, and he traveled all over the world. Simply put, he lived the life that most people only see in affluent magazines or ostentatious MTV music videos. While living in the lap of luxury, Dion was still always watching his back, so he could never quite get comfortable. His antennae would go up when deals went too smoothly or when someone new entered the fray. Was this person a cop? An informant? A murderer?

"That life has consequences," he says.

One of those consequential days came when Dion and a few friends ran low on product, so they turned to a different source than usual. Dion rarely stepped outside his main, trusted supplier, but a group in Denver claiming to have more than enough blow was intriguing. Dion and his partners knew of the Mile High City group, which was, in turn, aware of Dion's team. The Denver guys had done some selling in Ohio, but they were low-level players, at least outside of their home turf. Deciding to give the group a chance at partnership, Dion packed a haul of cash in a duffel bag to seal the deal and headed west to Denver in his Cadillac Seville.

After checking into a hotel and stashing about $300,000 in their room, Dion and two friends headed to a house via printed MapQuest directions to negotiate the deal.

Working with someone new was always a bit of a cat-and-mouse game, but those meetings sometimes amounted to stacks of cash for all involved. Dion's network was always so trusted that he never carried guns to drug deals, and he always refused to work with people who needed firearms. In Denver, he felt no different. No guns.

Within seconds of entering the house, Dion knew something was amiss because everything was happening too quickly and because everything was smooth. Dion had done enough deals to know that this didn't feel right. In that life, nothing ever goes seamlessly, and things went south quickly.

Just after pleasantries were exchanged, Dion and his two friends were bum rushed with guns pointed at them. The suppliers had turned into attackers, pushing Dion and his buddies to the ground and hogtying them with duct tape. The sheer panic was abundantly apparent, but Dion and his pals were in no position to fight back. They were outnumbered, outweaponed and out of their Ohio element.

The three men were shuffled into a nearby bedroom, where plastic tarps covered the carpet, similar to the drop cloths painters use for easy cleanup. If you've ever seen a Hollywood thriller, plastic bags are never a good sign and usually signal someone's death. Seeing their likely fates, Dion and his two cohorts were blindfolded and placed on their knees, execution style.

"Where's the money!" the attackers demanded to know.

Everything happened so fast that Dion didn't know how many attackers there were or even how many guns were pointed at him. Considering the most lethal thing Dion had on him was lip balm, one man with one gun was more than sufficient, though.

"Where's the fucking money!"

These men were serious about getting money, and Dion knew it. He didn't ask questions. Still hogtied and slumped over, he told the men where they could find the six-figure payday. He then wondered if he had uttered his final words.

Visions of his death creeping into his mind, as he heard shuffling around. He even though he heard the house door close, but wasn't sure if someone was leaving or entering. The sound of his Cadillac being driven away from the house was unmistakable, though. The men had taken it.

Still, Dion was alive. He was alive!

The sound of panting from himself and two friends filled the room, the hyperventilating and breathing so deep that it could fill a Macy's Day Parade balloon. Those were the only noises in the home, but there was still uncertainty about whether anyone else was there. With their eyesight taken away via the blindfold, it was possible that they were being watched by a silent assassin in the room.

After 20 minutes, Dion had waited long enough. Hoping he and his buddies were alone, he began working his way out of the sticky, gray duct tape and eventually succeeded. His adrenaline was at an all-time high when he took off the blindfold and looked around.

His eyes darted around the room. The coast was clear. Deciphering no movement in the house, he rushed to his buddies, removing their blindfolds and helping to untie them from their duct tape restraints. Not wanting to stick around for a cup of tea or retribution, they ran toward the home's entryway, twisted the gold-colored knob attached to the door and simultaneously pulled it open. Seeing no threat in sight, the three men, who felt like they were dead men walking just 30 minutes ago, scampered out of there with no car to flee to. It was snowing outside, but Dion was heated… and scared.

Rattled, walking through the brutal snowstorm and desperately hoping not to see their hostage takers, Dion told his friends, "We gotta get our asses back to Ohio."

Soon after finding safety, a friend wired money and Dion and his pals were on the first flight back to Dayton. They never returned to the hotel to see if their attackers retrieved the duffel bag of money.

If not, a housekeeper got a hell of a tip.

Despite the life-and-death incident in Denver, Dion continued his dealings for some time. But, as is usually the case with this felonious life, it all has to end somewhere.

"You just never know where trails are hot," he says of that life.

Dion was sound asleep on his plush pillow-top mattress when authorities came to his house to put him in handcuffs. His life of crime ended when he was convicted under the RICO Act, which is how the government took down many top-line mafia members in the '80s and '90s.

For the next eight years, a 6-foot by 8-foot prison cell was what Dion called home. The man who once had free rein in his city quickly found out he had no control over his environment in prison. He was told when to eat, sleep, wake up and urinate. Because he was educated, Dion worked primarily for the warden while in lockup, a far better gig than laundry or kitchen duty.

Upon his release in 2015, he was already turning his life around and had no plans to revert to his drug-carrying days. His baby daughter, born while he was incarcerated, was all that mattered to him.

Four Years Later

The radical change in Dion Green's post-prison life began on Memorial Day 2019.

It was a stunning day in Dayton, Ohio, one of those postcard days. The sun was out, the birds were chirping and the sky was spotted with a few high clouds that added to the mystique. For nearly two weeks, the Midwest, from border to border and corner to corner, had been getting battered by a tornado outbreak. "Tornado Alley," an unofficial geographical area that consists of parts of Texas, Oklahoma, Kansas, Nebraska, South Dakota, Missouri, Iowa and Minnesota, among others, had been mercilessly tortured with twisters day in and day out in mid-to-late May. Experts have long believed Tornado Alley is moving eastward toward Indiana and Michigan.

During the 14-day May 2019 outbreak, tornadoes were confirmed in 23 states. EF3 tornadoes, which the Enhanced Fujita scale says have wind gusts of 136-165 mph, touched down in 18 states. In all, 400 confirmed tornadoes were produced, and rainfall records were shattered across the region.

Until May 27, 2019, Ohio had largely been spared from the severe weather, with some exceptions.

While relaxing in his two-bedroom, two-bathroom home in North Dayton, the atmosphere changed. The sun had already set, but streetlights illuminated the roads. A steadily increasing wind gave residents an unsettled feeling, having seen what neighboring states had been suffering from over the past few weeks. The air, which had been crisp, quickly turned murky, and the dark sky began to resemble that of a horror film.

During moments of severe weather, such as tornadoes or hurricanes, it's common knowledge to stay away from windows and seek shelter. Dion, though, couldn't help himself, staring intently out the window and cautiously marveling at the rain and lightning engulfing his street. Around 10:45 p.m., his eyes widened when his neighbor's deep-rooted tree lifted from the ground and danced end-over-end down the street like an inflatable pool toy.

This was Dion's cue to grab his 10-year-old daughter, Niara, and his girlfriend, Donita, and take cover.

As lightning shrouded his home like a blanket, Dion and the family rushed downstairs, step after step. He then realized his dog Prince, an XL Bully, wasn't by his side, so he had to run back up the stairs to retrieve him.

The night was exceedingly getting more violent by the second.

While carrying Prince to the basement, a half mile-wide tornado barreled toward Dion's house. He heard the power grid go out as he reached the last stair, which led to his fully furnished basement. Normally, the family might be watching TV down there, but tonight was different.

Hunkered down in the darkness, Dion's house started moving, almost talking. Although he couldn't see much from below ground, he could hear his home being torn apart. Wood was being snapped like a matchstick. Shingles from the roof were lifting off the house, and the glass windows — the same ones Dion recently peered out of — were popping like kernels at a movie theater. If hell has a sound, this was it.

All he could do was cover Niara and Donita's heads in the corner of the room and hope the home's first floor didn't collapse on top of them.

The house stayed upright, but they weren't out of the woods. After one tornado was over, two more came.

Like a science experiment, the house that Dion bought in 2016 was being dissected, and he could do nothing about it. From his basement, Dion had to listen to his house disintegrate while EF4, EF3, and EF2 tornadoes spun Dayton on its head. Along the way, a gas station was flattened, family homes were exterminated, an apartment building was decimated and an elementary school's walls collapsed. May 27 turned out to be the most active day of the tornado outbreak, with 59 twisters, 15 of which hit the Dayton area.

It was still pitch-black outside when the storms subsided, so the extent of the damage to Dion's house wasn't totally realized. He knew it was bad. Really bad. He knew his roof was gone because he could see stars from his living room, almost like an unwanted camping trip.

As the sun started peeking out from the East and providing the first glimmer of daylight, Dion reluctantly walked out of his house to assess more damage. As expected, windows were shattered, the white clapboards had been torn off, 3/4 of the roof was gone, doors were off their hinges and the framework was crooked. You would have thought the house was uninhabited.

If Dion's home took a gut punch, the rest of his street took a knockout blow.

"Where are all the neighbors?" Dion wondered after seeing neighboring homes, once full of pictures, love and memories, turned into firewood overnight.

Months later, Dion's home was also reduced to debris, having been knocked down after being deemed unlivable. Dayton and its surrounding area suffered an estimated $500 million in damages.

August 3, 2019

It had been just over two months since the tornadoes ravaged Dayton when Dion Green got a phone call from a friend.

"Hey, let's go down to the water," the pal said, referring to Mad River, a 66-mile stream nearby known for canoeing and kayaking. Fishermen often descend on the river to reel in brown trout and rainbow trout.

Before losing his tornado-blighted home, Dion had spent hours and hours cleaning up and picking up debris. It was never-ending. It felt like Groundhog Day. He hadn't been off his street since the Memorial Day tornadoes.

"Nah, I have too much going on," he told his buddy. But, after thinking about it, he decided he needed a break, so Dion called his friend back and agreed to meet him. After all, he loves canoeing. Relaxing on the water is like a reset, something he certainly needed and deserved.

The day, Aug. 3, 2019, was going superbly. The river was calm, not too busy and the sky was a shade of Tiffany-blue. Dion embraced it all while sipping on his homemade "River Juice," a cold, slushy concoction of tequila, bourbon and Chick-fil-A lemonade.

"I needed this. I needed to feel alive again," Dion told his pal as the soft currents guided his canoe.

Toward the end of the day, Dion started thinking about his father, Derrick Fudge. Although Derrick wasn't around as much as Dion would have liked during childhood, the father and son had a tight relationship and hung out when time allowed. Derrick, 57, was a damn fine fisherman, a faithful bell ringer for the Salvation Army and a ridiculously good cornhole player, and Dion often played his father in the latter, rarely winning. Dion and Derrick were both card sharks and their arguments, all in love, were legendary — boy, did they argue.

Following a pristine day floating on the river, Dion decided to call his dad.

"You want to go to the Oregon District tonight," he asked, referring to the historic part of Dayton known for its restaurants, bars, food trucks and entertainment.

The Oregon District is somewhat of a town square for the locals looking to meet others, imbibe and bar hop. Rarely does the district pass on a chance to celebrate, be it for birthdays or bachelorette parties or any day that ends in "Y."

"Sure," Derrick answered the invitation to a night of revelry.

It had been a fun two-day stretch for Derrick. The day before Dion's overture, Derrick attended a family reunion in Springfield, Ohio. There, he spent the afternoon eating, laughing, talking about his beloved Pittsburgh Steelers and hanging out with his sister. He happily relayed his intentions to paint his granddaughter's bedroom for her birthday and help people whose homes were damaged by the tornadoes two months prior.

Now he was getting to hang out with his son and drink Jack Daniels at Newcom's bar? Things were clearly on the upswing.

Dubbing itself a "spirited establishment" and sitting across from the famed street-wide metal archway welcoming patrons to the area — the word "Oregon" runs the length of the facade — Newcom's is one of the hotspots of the Oregon District. Family-owned, the bar pays homage to Colonel George Newcom, one of Dayton's first settlers. In 1796, the Colonel and his wife, Mary, opened the original Newcom's Tavern, a log structure that operated both as a tavern and a hostel. The log cabin that housed the 18th-century tavern, which survived floods, multiple relocations and the War of 1812, is now in Dayton's Carillon Historical Park.

All these centuries later, at the new Newcom's, Derrick and Dion's night couldn't have gone any better. The place was bustling, as it usually is on a Saturday night. Night owls were buying drinks, and bartenders were mixing cocktails two or three at a time from the long bar that ran the length of the building. While Dion's sister, Megan, and her boyfriend went to the second level of the bar, Dion, Derrick and Donita drank in the environment from the street level. Amid the whiskeys (Dion only had one cocktail after a day of "River Juice"), the group chit-chatted and expressed disbelief and sadness about a horrific mass shooting that occurred 13 hours earlier in El Paso, Texas, which claimed the lives of 23 people.

The calendar flipped to Aug. 4, and Saturday night became Sunday morning, but none of that mattered to Derrick, who was dancing up a storm, so much so that a security guard asked the group to leave, which they agreed to do. It was late anyway, and Dion was growing weary from having been on the water all day. It was just after 1 a.m. when Dion and Co. decided to call it a night. After stowing their cell phones in their pockets and giving their drinks one last gulp, Derrick, Dion and Donita made their way to Newcom's heavy, black door and exited. Megan and her beau, however, remained upstairs in the club, and it was assumed that they weren't interested in leaving the bar yet. Dion casually stood beside a taco stand on the sidewalk for a second to soak in the evening, the first real one he'd had since the twisters destroyed his house.

The Oregon District was busy as the smell of cumin and carne asada wafted. While making their way East toward the car, Dion, Derrick, and Donita dodged people on the sidewalk like they were in a Frogger video game. It seemed everyone was letting loose, having been pent up for months following the tornadoes.

The threesome was about to pass a packed-to-the-gills bar called Blind Bob's when a tall, slender man walked around a corner near Ned Peppers Bar, directly across where the trio stood. He was wearing a mask and body armor. He was also carrying an AR-style pistol with a 100-round magazine.

POP, POP!

Two shots. Dion heard two loud pops but still didn't believe this was happening. An onslaught of bullets continued.

Having grown up around rough circumstances and put in sometimes perilous surroundings, Dion had been shot at twice before, but something about this was different.

For the next 30 seconds, the man fired 41 rounds into the crowded Oregon District at East 5th Street. People were taking cover on the ground, ducking behind cars or trying to run into a bar, any bar, many of which immediately shut and locked their doors at the sound of gunfire, Newcom's included. Dion, Donita and Derrick all dropped to the ground on the street in an attempt to evade the bullets that were being fired at a rate faster than one per second.

The shooter meandered through the small portion of the area, haphazardly shooting toward Newcom's and Blind Bob's. Bullets were altering life and damaging property as they slammed into people, buildings and cars.

A woman just a few feet from Dion screamed after taking a bullet.

This was real. This was happening.

As Dion looked up from the ground, the shooter, a 24-year-old man, was crossing the street and coming directly toward him. Rounds were flying over the top of his prone body. Undeterred, the gunman walked past Dion and stepped over Derrick. A woman in front of them, who turned out to be the shooter's sister, was dead.

It was chaos in every sense of the word, and people ran in all directions.

"Dad," Dion said after the gunfire stopped, "get up, we gotta get out of here now! Get up!"

Derrick wasn't moving or making a sound, but Dion thought his dad didn't hear him amid the hysteria.

"Dad, we're outta here! Everyone, get outta here!"

Still, Derrick, lying on his back on East 5th Street, wasn't moving. He was breathing but not moving.

Knowing this wasn't normal, Dion leaned down next to his dad, whose eyes were open and looking like he'd been in shock. Being in shock was one thing; being shot was another.

With his phone in his right hand, Dion turned on the flashlight function and shined it on his dad's chest to get a better look. He didn't see any blood, which was good news. He then angled the flashlight to shine on Derrick's head and shoulder. A puddle of blood had already formed on the pavement. Derrick had been shot five times, but somehow, Dion and his girlfriend, both of whom were shoulder to shoulder with Derrick, were physically unharmed.

Derrick's body shielded his son from the shots.

As blood oozed out of his father, Dion immediately found himself doing chest compressions on his dad.

"Get up! Come on! Get up!"

Time seemed like it was standing still. Despite the screams and stampeding enveloping him, Dion could only hear silence, his dad's silence.

Derrick's lips quivered as if he were trying to speak, but words weren't coming out of his mouth, akin to a fish out of water.

Dion didn't want to accept the reality, but he knew his dad was fading fast and past the point of no return. Rather than continue CPR, he got down, wrapped his arms around his father and lay on top of him. Dion clung to him like Velcro, refusing to let go or let anyone touch them.

"I love you, Dad. Please get up. I love you. I love you," he kept repeating, his emotions pouring out. He could taste the salinity from the tears that had rolled down his face onto his lips.

Dion was breaking down. Derrick, meanwhile, stayed down.

Derrick died right there on the street in his son's blood-soaked arms. Eight other innocent people lost their lives that evening, too.

To this day, Dion struggles with survivor's guilt.

"I don't know why that man didn't kill me. That's something that I deal with every day."

The entire incident lasted 32 seconds — police who were on regular patrol of the Oregon District engaged the shooter just 20 seconds into the killing spree. The gunman's life ended after law enforcement hit him with 30 rounds. Police later determined that the gunman fired 41 shots, five of which hit Derrick.

Mid-September 2019

Six weeks after the Dayton shooting, Dion came into Mary Jo's life as she accompanied Tommy Maher to Ohio for one of his "honor trips." Tommy and Mary Jo had no plans to meet with the families of the Dayton shooting, as they just wanted to do some random acts of kindness there and be on their way. During their stay, Dion discovered Tommy and reached out.

"Hey, this kid wants to meet with me," Tommy told Mary Jo as they sat down for dinner. Of course, Tommy had done deep research on the Dayton shooting and already knew a lot about the victims and survivors.

Her eyes widened as Tommy spoke about Dion, and Mary Jo began having a mini panic attack at the table of the restaurant, located within earshot of the shooting site. Most residents had yet to return to the area.

"I don't want to talk to another family member," she said, flabbergasted. "I don't want to do that. What do I have in common with him?"

In her mind, this kid was almost 20 years her junior, from Middle America and had a very different upbringing.

Although the shooting had been weeks ago, Dayton was still somber. Residents hadn't forgotten what happened there.

"Listen," Tommy implored, "stay for a little bit, and if you're not comfortable, say you're going to go to the bathroom and just leave. Don't make a big scene."

At parties, that's called an "Irish Goodbye." Conveniently enough, they were meeting at an Irish pub, too. Mary Jo was already planning her exit.

While sitting at their nondescript table at the Dublin Pub, in walked a well-dressed Black man. He introduced himself as Dion Green and began speaking about his situation with remarkable eloquence. He described the night his dad died, which was sickening. He spoke of family members he and his father rarely spoke to, trying to get money from a GoFundMe that had been set up, which was also sickening. People were coming out of the woodwork in the name of the all-mighty dollar bill, people Dion had never heard of. Scammers, all of them. As Dion had appeared on several local and national news outlets at that point, some people wanted both his new platform and money. Mary Jo dealt with similar things after Kurt's passing, so she suddenly found herself sharing her story and imparting whatever advice she could.

So much for that Irish Goodbye.

Without blinking, Mary Jo gave Dion her phone number and email. The two had both lost a loved one before their very eyes, an unfortunate bond they share.

"Everything you're dealing with, I've been there. Call me if you need anyone to talk to who understands."

Despite Tommy arranging the meeting, he mostly sat silently beside Mary Jo, eating his dinner. Clearly, there was a method to his madness.

Since that day, Dion and MaryJo have chatted fairly frequently.

"I'm glad I never had to 'go to the bathroom' that night," she smirks. "I've used the Irish goodbye many other times, just not with Dion."

October 2019

Dion Green was emotionally lost for weeks. He thought about his dad daily. He thought about that fateful night daily.

"If I never called him, he would be here," he sometimes thought.

The "if only" game is natural, but it's also perilous because the reality is that the ending doesn't change.

In Dion's world, so many things had to be done: he had to help clear out his dad's house, close his bank account, shut off the utilities and pay Derrick's final bills. There were so many things he never thought he would have to do. When his father's burial costs proved to be rather substantial, he applied for victim's compensation via the Victims of Crime Act (VOCA), which he thought would be automatic considering the circumstances of his dad's death. Instead, he was greeted by a letter of denial because Derrick had a 2011 felony drug conviction. It didn't matter to the state of Ohio that Derrick served his time and turned his life around. There was no gray area here. This was black and white, an open-and-shut case.

Dion's denial letter came before his father was even buried, prompting him to tear it up upon receiving it.

Created in 1984 as a way to financially assist victims of crime, funding for the Crime Victims Fund, known as VOCA, comes from federal crime fines and forfeitures, not taxpayer dollars. Funds are then distributed to states annually. Many states have different mechanisms for distributing the money. Victims of violent crime are supposed to get priority. As of May 2024, the Crime Victims Fund balance was over $1.5 billion. In 2019, the year Derrick was shot, just under $394 million was paid to victim compensation advocates — of that, more than $52 million went to just funeral costs.

VOCA denials can come for a variety of reasons, including an application being filled out incorrectly or outside a specific time frame. In Derrick's case, his denial came because he hadn't been 10 years removed from his drug arrest. He led a life on the straight and narrow and had a clean record for nine years and six months, but Ohio required an entire decade of total lawfulness.

The application for VOCA funding can be distasteful, invasive and poorly timed; applicants are asked about their income and details of their lives on the heels of suddenly losing a loved one via violence.

As if losing his dad wasn't enough, the VOCA denial opened up a different compartment of trauma for Dion, which he felt was dangerous, as untreated trauma can have damaging effects.

Disgusted by the process, Dion couldn't just stand by. His dad did nothing wrong on Aug. 4. Derrick served time behind bars and paid his debt to society for his crime. Why should he be penalized when so many others weren't?

While not hiding his anger at the law, Dion delved deeply into VOCA law (he essentially has a Ph.D. in it) and began lobbying the Ohio legislature. He spoke passionately to representatives about VOCA and did dozens of media interviews about problems with the law. Obstacles need to be eased, and reform is needed, he insisted to anyone listening.

Standing before the lawmakers, Dion said, "Once again, like many of us survivors or victims, we are the ones living day to day with PTSD and trauma in our lives, and without proper resources or funds to help individuals get the resources they need is crucial. Mental health is a key component to many survivors because it is a step to recovery and healing, but if a survivor cannot afford these services, they are left suffering from trauma that can become dangerous to themselves and others.

"But I just want you to really consider the impact this can have too many survivors who are able to retain these funds, but also the effect it has on the people who are not able to get the help they need."

Following years of pleading and arguing before lawmakers, Dion sat in the gallery and watched the Senate Judiciary Committee pass Senate Bill 36 in November 2020. A few months later, the full Senate voted to expand victims' access to compensation. Then, in December 2021, Ohio Gov. Mike DeWine signed the bill into law. It became active the following March.

"This would not have been possible without the countless survivors who made their voices heard and made it clear that true safety isn't possible without addressing trauma in our communities," Sen. Nathan Manning, one of the bill's sponsors, said afterward, referring to Dion.

The Dayton Daily News called Dion a "community gem." He told the newspaper: "My ultimate goal is for survivors to step into their voice because our voice is powerful." The city's ABC affiliate hailed him as a "hometown hero."

In 2021, then-President Joe Biden signed the VOCA Fix to Sustain the Crime Victims Fund Act, which provided assistance for crime victims, including counseling expenses, medical bills and lost wages. In an overwhelming vote, the House of Representatives passed the bill with a vote of 384-38. In this day and age, it doesn't get more bipartisan than that. Lawmakers from both sides of the aisle stood behind the president to watch him sign the necessary paperwork.

Although Dion wasn't in the Oval Office for that occasion, he's often in Washington, D.C., and at the White House due to work with the Office of Gun Violence Prevention. He also now sits on a smattering of national boards centered on crime survivors. Since the shooting, he's been a proponent of banning assault weapons federally and spoke before the Supreme Court in 2021 during NYSRPA v. Bruen, a Second Amendment-centric case. (The court eventually ruled that New York's law requiring a license to carry a concealed weapon was unconstitutional.)

Spurred by his father's death and his own experiences, Dion not only penned a memoir called *Untitled: Act of God.*

Act of Man, but he also launched his FUDGE Foundation nonprofit in 2020 to help those impacted by violence, be it gun violence, domestic violence or otherwise. The nonprofit, whose full name is Flourishing Under Distress Given Encouragement, i.e., FUDGE, supports those in times of grief from traumatic events by connecting people to resources, such as counseling or burial services, something few people are prepared for following violent, fatal incidents. Through FUDGE, he has also set up a seven-week program for predominantly at-risk, fatherless kids and helps them with self-awareness and self-love.

Devon Stargent, Dion's childhood neighbor, has seen the mentorship firsthand.

"He's really a father figure to these kids," Devon noted.

Dion and Devon have known each other for years, but their friendship started on the wrong foot. Their first-ever encounter came Devon called Dion's sister a cruel name, sending her to tears. Upon telling her sibling, Dion marched straight over to Devon and was fully prepared to give him a beating.

A fight never ensued, but Devon realized Dion was always willing to stand up for others and protect them. This principle applies to the mentees at FUDGE. It's not uncommon for some of these kids, most of them teenagers, to have juvenile records. Dion, of course, can relate to the kids, considering his past. He also shows the kids a better way, hoping they'll eschew the criminal life that once consumed him.

Dion Green walked so these kids could run.

For seven weeks, Dion guides the teens as they participate in food drives and community support projects. They learn to collaborate and rely on each other. Due to this setup, kids who initially start as enemies often become best friends. That's by design.

FUDGE isn't a "scared straight" program but more of a friendly boot camp.

"The main goal is to end gun violence, and you have to start with the child and their way of thinking because these are the leaders and the people of the future," Devon said. "Dion is a leader among leaders."

Sabrina Jordan became fast friends with Dion after the Oregon District shooting, and they had something in common: they both lost loved ones to gun violence.

"Anytime I'm going down that dark path, he comes and checks on me, talks to me, wants to get me out of the house," she said of Dion. "We just talk. We do a lot of laughing with each other."

Sabrina has her triggers, having lost two sons to guns — Jamal McShann, 22, died in an October 2013 shooting; Jamarco McShann, 22, died almost four years later to the day at the hands of police, who claimed he pointed a gun at officers first. Sabrina believes her son posed no threat and argues the police deliberately killed him and covered it up.

Following Jamarco's 2017 shooting, Sabrina founded the Ohio Families Unite Against Police Brutality, whose mission is pretty self-explanatory.

Sabrina and Dion met in 2019 after attending one of his speeches, in which he advocated for the end of gun violence. Since then, they've helped similarly minded people register to vote and collaborated on multiple Dayton community events, most of which Dion funds from his own pocket.

A self-described "very impatient person," Sabrina believes Dion is a levelheaded force in her corner.

"Sometimes he has to whisper in my ear just to calm down and chill out because I'm very outspoken," she says.

Ironically, she sees Dion as a little brother, whereas the kids of his FUDGE program see him as a father figure. It's all family, and everyone marvels at Dion for different reasons.

"Dion," Sabrina once said, "I can't keep up with you. Where do you get this energy?"

"From living."

FUDGE billboards and signs are not uncommon in Dayton, all of them stating: "When is enough! Enough!" They all condemn gun violence and demand change.

"The reason the FUDGE Foundation was created stems back to VOCA," Dion says. "So many people like myself were denied funding. I thought, if this is happening here, then this is happening across the country."

Through the foundation, Dion found himself pushing for reform and advocating for gun victims in Nashville, Maine, upstate New York, Texas, and others.

He's not averse to giving gun violence victims money from his own pocket. It was via the FUDGE Foundation that he was able to provide that $10,000 reward for Kason Thomas's safe return after his abduction.

Federal and state resources are almost always available immediately after a mass trauma event, but they're gone within weeks, sometimes before survivors can even start to process what happened. With FUDGE, Dion bridges that gap and offers support for as long as people need it. He is now a certified peer support specialist and a social worker at his own counseling practice.

"I just started being a voice and showing up and being intentional," he says of the early FUDGE days. "That right there was opening doors. I am a survivor, but in the midst of everything going on, I was able to put my pain to the side to be able to help another person going through theirs. They don't know how to navigate through it."

Dion Green isn't going to be quiet. He wants someone to pay for his father's death. Someone needs to be culpable. Yes, the gunman is the obvious choice, but he's dead. The company that, in his mind, made all the Oregon District killings possible is just as much at fault.

"We need to hold this company accountable," he said, referring to Kyung Chang Industry USA, the manufacturer of the large-capacity magazine the shooter used in the Dayton attacks. The drums that Kyung Chang Industry (KCI) makes hold 100 bullets at a time and allow shooters to continue firing without having to pause to reload. Magazines often jut out from the bottom of a rifle. They're small, often lightweight, affordable, very readily available and do exactly what they're intended to do: let shooters fire bullets incredibly quickly.

That night, the shooter, his sister and a mutual friend went to the popular area in the family car. For over an hour, the gunman hung out at a bar unremarkably and raised no concern. After being separated from his sister and friend at the bar, the shooter casually went to the silver sedan and grabbed his body armor, an AR-15 assault-style rifle and a KCI-made large-capacity magazine, which stored and fed ammunition into the gun.

The Dayton police chief said the shooter had 250 rounds of ammunition, all easily available to him because of the magazine.

"It is fundamentally problematic. To have that level of weaponry in a civilian environment, unregulated, is problematic," then-Police Chief Richard Biehl said in a press conference afterward.

Like in Dayton, large-capacity magazines, or LCM's, were used in some of the United States' largest shootings, including those at Columbine High School in 1999 and Sandy Hook Elementary School in 2012.

To Dion, the police chief hit the nail on the head, and in August 2021, he and several others who lost family members in the Oregon District filed a lawsuit against Kyung Chang Industry. The lawsuit was filed in Clark County, Nevada, where KCI's U.S. operations are based — their offices are 11 miles from where a man shot Mary Jo's husband using a gun equipped with a high-capacity magazine. In Vegas, the man who killed Kurt von Tillow had 12 100-round magazines.

The lawsuit's opening words come from firearms manufacturer and designer William B. Ruger, Sr., who claimed, "No honest man needs more than 10 rounds."

In the 93-page complaint, lawyers representing Dion and four other families argued that LCM's are "not necessary for lawful self-defense or hunting. They are necessary for killing large numbers of people quickly, before the user can be stopped."

"While soldiers in war may need to shoot many people quickly in battle, civilians need LCMs only to engage in mass assaults on other civilians or law enforcement—that is, mass shootings," it continued, calling KCI's manufacturing of 100-round magazines "reckless."

To be clear, Dion and the four other families aren't arguing to restrict someone's 2nd Amendment rights, but they are steadfast that law-abiding citizens have no reason to shoot 100 rounds in under a minute. Safeguards should be in place, the parties argued, via Ohio-based attorney Ben Cooper. Better mental health services would be one safeguard, as would red-flag laws, the lawsuit argues, but Dion firmly believes that limiting magazine capacity sizes could be the first step — a huge step — in lessening the body count in gun-related mass tragedies.

A first of its kind, no lawsuit had ever been brought forth focused solely on the marketing, manufacturing and sale of high-capacity magazines. Many lawsuits have been filed against gun manufacturers and sellers, and there have been unsuccessful challenges to magazine capacity itself, but Dion's magazine-intense lawsuit is believed to be more specific than those. In the legal paperwork, a photo of the actual Dayton shooter's gun and magazine is included. The haunting image of unfired rounds was plainly visible in the magazine.

Just two weeks before the lawsuit was filed, KCI USA posted a picture to its website and social media of an assault rifle with a 100-round LCM. The caption alongside the image read: "Keeping it 100."

This was like rubbing salt in the wounds of people like Dion, who argues that the manufacturing company's business is despicable and should be shunned by ordinary, decent people. Keeping drums to a sensible limit can be the difference between life and death.

Richard, the aforementioned former top cop in Dayton, told the Washington Post in 2023: "If he was using a 30-round magazine, he would at least have to reload once. A 15-round magazine, he would reload twice. That could be six lives saved in that particular incident. That's why I think it matters."

Any pause in a shooting allows people to escape. During the Vegas shooting, many of the attendees of the Route 91 Festival spoke about running from the grounds during a break in the gunfire (one of them being the author of this book).

Although there's no limit on the number of rounds a magazine can hold, 100 is quite high. The industry standard is 30.

No matter when the case against KCI goes to court, Dion will be front and center.

"Whatever transpires or whether we bring attention, whether we create change, I'm here for the long run," he says. "I know it's going to be a long process, and I'm going to keep fighting against it."

CHAPTER 6

Tony Burditus

He was in his military fatigues, watching his unit clear a small village in Iraq. The sun was shining and the day was so clear that you could see for miles. As a member of the Army's Special Forces, Tony Burditus had done several tours in the Middle East and was lucky enough to have avoided gunfire during Operation Iraqi Freedom. That day, 17 years into his military career in the open desert of the Republic of Iraq, things changed.

With his colleague Aaron by his side, Tony focused on soldiers from the Iraqi partner force clearing out a windowless abandoned home, which seemed rather harmless. The house's four exterior walls had been weathered by the relentless heat in the Samawah desert, where temperatures can reach 125 degrees. The few interior walls weren't in much better shape, as they were crumbling like a two-day-old muffin. Tony and Aaron, his medic, were even less protected as they stood out in the open air, monitoring and instructing the unit. Still, danger didn't exactly seem imminent as the two watched fellow Special Forces guys clear the dismantled village, which was nothing more than an unsung, typical task. Tony had been deployed to Iraq twice for a year at a time, and this type of work wasn't uncommon.

This was the boring, tedious work that doesn't garner headlines, and rightfully so.

The silence of the day was soon interrupted as automatic gunfire started peppering the area, and no one seemed to know where it was coming from. Bullets were smacking off buildings, punishing the ground, whizzing by Tony and Aaron and loudly clanking off a chain-link fence behind them. Their response: laughter.

"Oh shit," Aaron said, not moving a muscle.

Tony, meanwhile, couldn't respond, giggling as if he were watching a standup comedian perform.

There's a scene in *Pulp Fiction* where John Travolta and Samuel L. Jackson's characters nonchalantly stand silently unconcerned as a 20-something man unloads a revolver in their direction. The characters didn't seem fazed despite the fact that one bullet could have quickly taken their lives. The scene in the movie took place in an apartment, whereas Tony's situation occurred in a war zone and was a real-life experience. Still, Tony's reaction to the incoming gunfire was eerily similar to that of John Travolta's character.

Still unable to control their emotions from the sneak attack, the men retreated toward an adjacent well house used for water storage. The well house, their only protection in that split second, sat next to a canal flanked by palm trees and shrubbery, which is not exactly the vision you conjure up when thinking about Iraq. When people lived in the village in better times, they planted vegetation to beautify the surroundings. During the more serene times, before the Saddam Hussein regime, water wasn't in short supply either, as the area was covered with irrigation ditches. During the Iraq War, which ranged from 2003 to 2011, water had largely dried up. It was about as desolate as desolate could be. Coincidentally, it wasn't rare to have these vegetation plots in the middle of the desert throughout the country. These grass strips were essentially survivors of the war.

Hunkered down and protected by the well house structure, Tony and Aaron continued to chuckle like they were keen on an inside joke. Headquarters needed to be alerted, but they also knew the wartime commanders at Victory Base Complex headquarters wouldn't take kindly to the sudden Abbott and Costello offering.

"Pull it together, pull it together," Tony urged while smiling. "We have to call this in."

After collecting himself, Tony was able to call in the threat, which turned out to be a father and two adult sons firing at U.S. soldiers and their Iraqi counterparts from a nearby ditch. An aerial team quickly eliminated the threat, having spotted the father in a ditch with his machine gun; his sons had squirted up the canal, but they were taken out from above by an Apache helicopter.

Years later and long after Tony retired from the Army, which included a deployment to Afghanistan's western provinces during Operation Enduring Freedom, he can think back to other times he was shot at during wartime, but that's the closest he came to being the primary target of gunfire. Movies make the military out to be something it's not. More often than not, soldiers don't experience life-and-death situations in real-time, no more so than driving a car on any U.S. interstate. However, for a handful of military men and women, especially the elite units, gunfire is simply an occupational hazard. Considering Tony worked as one of the most highly skilled soldiers in the world for 26 and a half years, you would safely assume that the threat of being fired upon was over after his retirement. You would be wrong.

Denise Salmon knew who Tony Burditus was in Hedgesville Middle School, but she wasn't entirely interested. He was a year older than her and seemed to have a wild lifestyle. They were total opposites. Tony was a skinny skateboarder whose grades were nowhere near valedictorian status. Not only was Tony not a straight-A student, he wasn't a straight-B student.

Straight-C was even pushing it. He was more of a just-enough-to-pass-this-class student. Denise, meanwhile, was a teacher's dream and a goodie-two-shoes. She was a hard worker, but could get an A without trying. Additionally, she came from a devoutly religious family, a stark contrast to Tony, who essentially adhered to the Golden Rule: Do unto others as you would have them do unto you. He was more of a country music guy, and Denise couldn't stop singing "Don't Stop Believing" by Journey. God, she was always singing that damn song.

"You were a cute kid in middle school," she told Tony years later, proving his Hedgesville High existence wasn't totally lost on her.

It was hard to be totally oblivious to anyone in Martinsburg, West Virginia, in the late '70s. With a population of about 14,000, the town wasn't a metropolitan area but much more of a farming community. With just under seven square miles of total land, Martinsburg had a small-town mentality. For some, there was an unspoken dress code of boots, jeans and a T-shirt, for others, a blouse and fashionable pants. Fashion was widely acceptable.

Located on the far eastern panhandle of West Virginia, the town is about a 30-minute drive to the Maryland border and only 90 minutes away from Washington, D.C. An oddity, it's actually closer to the state capitals of Pennsylvania, Maryland, Delaware, Virginia and New Jersey than it is to Charleston, the capital of West Virginia. Perhaps surprising to many, agriculture has been a fixture in West Virginia since the 1800s, and Martinsburg is the epicenter of the state's apple production. In fact, the area's Golden Delicious apples are sold in grocery stores up and down the East Coast. So proud the area is of its fruit, a giant time capsule statue of an apple was "planted" in downtown Martinsburg in 1990, and it's set to be opened in 2040. When Tony and Denise were growing up, orchards overwhelmed the landscape, but urban growth has unfortunately taken its toll on the number of apples now being produced.

As a youngster, Tony began working at the Rosemary Orchard, first operating behind the scenes in the warehouse, packing apples and peaches. He would later transition to driving tractors in the field. A good employee, he worked at the orchard until high school graduation. Oftentimes, while driving tractors out in the fields, the teenager would think about Denise, whom he started dating, having finally caught her attention in the hallways of Hedgesville High School during the latter years.

With the money earned from the orchard, Tony showered Denise with affection and loved spending money on her, despite his minimum wage salary. Since Tony still lived at home with his parents, his bills were minimal, although continually gassing up his car ate into his bottom line. Still, by high school kid standards, he was downright rich!

Life was fun, simple, and exciting. The world, however, had a funny way of bringing them back down to earth.

"Tony, I'm pregnant," Denise, then just 17, told her boyfriend, who had just graduated from Hedgesville.

"What? Pregnant? Are you sure? How do you know?" a flummoxed Tony wondered while internally knowing it was true. Still, Tony was confused and stunned. Hell, they'd only had sex once.

Denise, turns out, lost her virginity and got pregnant all in one fell swoop.

Pregnancy or not, Tony's commitment to Denise was unshakeable. That tall, lanky cowboy knew Denise was "the one" before he was even of legal voting age, but that's not to say they weren't overwhelmed.

"How are we going to do this?" the dad-to-be wondered.

While Tony figured out how to pay for a child, Denise went through a portion of her senior year of high school, eating for two. Then, in February of 1985, Denise and Tony welcomed their son, Joshua.

In the blink of an eye, they were teenage parents: teen mom and teen dad vs. the world. Neither had any international experience, but their son was their world. Everything revolved around him and his needs.

Once their duo became a trio, Tony knew what his next step would be. Denise had been away on a class trip for a few days, which gave Tony plenty of time to think. He needed to show Denise how devoted he was. Not only that, but he also wanted to show Denise how devoted he was.

After gassing up his car, Tony headed to the local nursery, snagged some roses and prepared to be about as romantic as any teenager could be. He was nervous — after all, he was still basically a glorified kid at this point — but Tony was sure that his next question was the right one.

"Let's get married," he told her in the seat of his two-door Ford after scooping up his lady love from the high school parking lot.

Following his question, er statement, the mother of his child said yes, not hesitating.

Just three months later, Denise Salmon became Denise Burditus — She and Tony tied the knot in a small ceremony in a local church before friends and family. In keeping with their simple lifestyle, Denise eschewed a traditional wedding gown, opting instead for a beautiful but understated dress, and Tony wore a suit, not a formal tuxedo.

In 1985 alone, Denise welcomed her son, graduated high school, got engaged and married. And, just two years after that, they welcomed a daughter, Mallorie.

"We did things a little backward," Tony acknowledged unapologetically.

First comes love, then comes marriage, then comes baby in the baby carriage? Not in Tony and Denise's world.

There was no shortage of love in the home. Money, however, was another story. To make ends meet, Tony made a difficult decision to leave the orchard because he was struggling financially. In a complete job 180, he went from working outdoors under Mother Nature's watchful eye to wasting away for Texas Stock Tab, where he worked from midnight to 8 am for four years.

A company with no real use these days, Texas Stock Tab produced continuous paper for computer printing, the kind with holes on the sides that had to be fed into a dot matrix printer, which was the norm in the 1980s and 1990s. With continuous paper, the sprocket holes (the holes on the sides) would be fed into the printer via rollers inside the machine. Pre-manufactured perforations allowed customers to easily remove the holes, leaving a clean 8x10 sheet of paper. It wasn't uncommon for perforations to rip uncleanly, though, causing too many imperfect homework and work assignments. With the advent of modern-day printers, continuous paper became archaic and went the way of the dinosaurs.

Tony hated the graveyard shift hours and wasn't passionate about the gig. By the time he'd get home in the morning from his unfulfilling computer-adjacent job, Denise was already long gone and posted up at the local bank where she worked. The kids were with Denise's mother, who basically provided free daycare. He was sleeping all day and working all night.

The schedule wore on Tony. He was missing his children growing up, and he was missing Denise. Their schedules didn't leave much overlapping, just a couple of hours here and there. Plus, once again, finances were dwindling. The computer gig paid better than the orchard, but upward movement and pay raises weren't happening. Amid this, Tony had met multiple military recruiters who promised him a better life. That life was more virtuous and had much better benefits, but he knew it meant time away from the family, to which he was unfortunately already getting accustomed. Still, he didn't dismiss the idea, and his sleep would suffer because of it.

Tenacious as ever, an Army recruiter called Tony consistently at 8:30 in the morning just as he was lying in bed after long, hard mornings at the paper mill.

Monday at 8:30 a.m.: *ring, ring, ring.*

Tuesday at 8:30 a.m.: *ring, ring.*

Wednesday at 8:30 a.m.: *ring, ring ring.*

It didn't stop.

"Don't call me," a heavy-eyed Tony said while picking up one day, "I'll call you when and if I'm ready."

By 1989, Tony knew that he wouldn't get anywhere working 80 hours a week in his tech-ish job, and he made the call.

"I told you I'd call you when I was ready, and I'm ready," he told the recruiter in his signature country drawl.

The recruiter could sense the determination.

"This isn't just your job, Tony. Being an Army wife is a job in and of itself."

"Denise is fully supportive of this."

Military life was always on the table in the Burditus home. Tony and Denise often had open conversations about him enlisting, and she never got in the way of her husband's dream. She always knew he could make something of himself and find his foothold. His calling card, she thought, might actually be an Army man.

Growing up in a typical three-bedroom home, Tony lost count of how often he'd watch *The Green Berets*, a John Wayne film set in South Vietnam. In the movie, the legendary actor's character commanded a team of Green Berets who defended a base and eventually captured a high-level Viet Cong officer. In Tony's mind, based strictly on the film, everyone in the Army had the same job — everyone shot guns and took out the enemy.

When Tony reported to basic training at Fort Dix in Trenton, New Jersey, he discovered his job wasn't worthy of box office glory. In his first four years working for Uncle Sam, Private Burditus was driving trucks from point A to B for the Army, and he was miserable. An Army Uber. Sure, it put food on the table for his family, but this was hardly what he envisioned. Low motivation was a common thread within that particular unit. Wanting to be more active and genuinely love his job, he yearned to be challenged. Soon after, a friend recommended that Tony go to Special Forces Selection, which is how this former orchard worker from eastern West Virginia ended up at the infamous Fort Bragg in North Carolina.

One of the largest military bases in the world, Fort Bragg, now called Fort Liberty, is often romanticized in pop culture. It's home to some of the most prestigious Army units, including the XVIII Airborne Corps, which played a huge role in the Battle of the Bulge in WWII. Several men stationed at Fort Bragg have gone on to work at the White House, CIA and NASA. There's even a movie being filmed called *Incident at Fort Bragg,* which is based on an alleged true story of an Irish priest being brought in to perform a sanctioned exorcism on a young soldier. The military claims this never happened. Hollywood says otherwise.

For three weeks at the base, Tony and his fellow Special Forces hopefuls were tested physically, mentally, emotionally and drowsily. Sleep deprivation was real. His will and soul were being tested. To prove his mettle, Tony had to run with a backpack full of heavy rocks or navigate out of a forest in the middle of the night with nothing but a compass and a map. It was hell. Absolute hell. Guys were dropping out of the program left and right — one guy in Tony's unit quit on Day 1.

"You'd wake up and people just weren't there anymore, and all their shit was gone," he recalled.

In 2009, a documentary called *Two Weeks of Hell* followed men vying to become Special Forces. When Tony went through the rigors of "special forces assessment and selection," as it's formally called, it was three weeks of hell. Kids these days have it easy… comparatively speaking.

Eventually, Tony became a communication sergeant within the Army Special Forces, better known as the Green Berets. In addition to being a combat expert, he's trained as a swimmer, paratrooper and survival expert.

John Wayne and Tony Burditus. Two peas in a pod. The former, however, was an actor. The latter is a certified badass.

At the time of Tony's acceptance into the elite fraternity, Morse Code — an alphabetic language from the early 19th century made up of dots and dashes — was still being used, so he learned how to read and encrypt this maddening language. Morse code was used heavily in World War I and World War II, and a handful of Air Force airmen still learn it today. In WWII, three dots and a dash —Morse code for the letter V — were used often, as it stood for "victory." A lot of three dots and a dash happened in WWII.

For the next 20 years, Tony was stationed in North Carolina's Fort Bragg, Washington's Fort Lewis, Torii Station in Okinawa, Japan, and the Yuma Proving Ground in Arizona. Denise and the kids usually relocated with him. Year-long deployments to Iraq and Afghanistan, both active war zones, weren't out of the norm. Many things that occurred out there aren't necessarily classified, but they're very much on a need-to-know basis. Tony is unassuming about it all. Probably because of movies, there's often an idea that Special Forces is all about kicking in doors and pulling triggers, but much of what Tony did was humanitarian work.

"We were trying to get communities back," he said.

While he was more "boots on the ground" in Iraq than in Afghanistan, the endgame was the same, which was getting infrastructure back into these ravaged communities and villages.

Throughout it all, Denise, the backbone of the family, supported him.

"I've never seen anyone manage a household like my mother did," said daughter Mallorie.

In some ways, Denise was a single mother — not in the traditional sense, of course, but there were lengthy spans where she took care of the kids 100% of the time. With Tony often deployed, Denise and her children developed a close, close bond, and they did everything together, be it camping, going to the movies, or driving in the car, belting out hits by Travis Tritt, Coolio and, obviously, Journey. Denise had more range than a golf course! While living in Washington, they'd pack up the car and spend the day at a three-story mall in Portland. To the delight of her kids, Denise was very, very fun to shop with.

"She hardly ever said no," Mallorie said.

But, when it came to her own fashion, Denise was much more focused on one thing: leggings. The family affectionately — or maybe not so affectionately — called them "fancy pants."

For a stretch of four years, you would be hard-pressed to find Denise without bright, bold leggings. Sure, she dressed professionally while working at the bank, but it was leggings time every other moment. She'd dress up her floral patterned "fancy pants" with boots, or she'd pair her bright green fancy pants with a jean jacket. Completing every outfit was a scarf. She pulled it off every time and seemed to have a never-ending inventory of leggings.

Denise wasn't perfect, but she was perfect for Tony. She was loyal, witty and kept him well fed… even if her cooking was unconventional.

"How about some of that chicken shit," Tony sometimes said, referring to a meal consisting of broccoli cheddar soup, vegetables, rice and chicken.

She would always combine the oddest things and make them for dinner, and Tony ate them up every time. Still, "chicken shit" was his favorite.

While Tony is the strong, silent type, nothing rattled his wife. She was also anything but silent or subtle. One time, Mallorie brought a guy home to meet the parents. She was interested in the guy and thought it was time for him to see the family dynamic.

In the living room, Tony sat in his reclining chair and began the evening by peppering the lad with somewhat innocuous questions, many of the "Where are you from?" and "What do you do?" variety.

"What's your credit score?" Denise chimed in.

"Mom!" an embarrassed and mortified Mallorie interrupted.

"These things are important," her mother protested. Again, hardly subtle.

Things never worked out between Mallorie and that guy, his credit score notwithstanding.

The mother-daughter duo was fiercely close. Denise was in the delivery room at Madigan Army Medical Center when Mallorie welcomed her first son, Konnor. Denise, about to become a new grandma, even held Konnor's leg while he was born.

Grandma and grandson were best friends. That was her boy. They wanted to do everything together. Mallorie has tried to recreate her mom's spaghetti squash because Konnor loved it, but she still can't get it right. Again, her cooking was delicious and unconventional.

There's no doubt that Tony had a difficult job and was literally putting his life on the line every time he walked out the door, but Denise's job was much, much harder. Tony's mother often reiterated that being a Green Beret was tough, no doubt, but being a military wife was not for the faint of heart. Denise's job was tougher than Tony's, to which he agreed.

"She handled every problem while I was gone and probably every problem while I was home, too," he says.

While Tony played G.I. Joe in the Middle East, Denise carved her own path and was a rockstar in her field. A wiz with numbers, Denise began working in banking before Tony even joined the military and stayed in that lane throughout his career. When the family lived outside of Tacoma, Washington, at Fort Lewis, she even had her own branch and worked her way up to Assistant Vice President at Heritage Bank. Denise continued to work there while Tony lived in an RV on the Arizona military base, but they were by no means distant, as they saw each other often and spoke daily via the phone, email and FaceTime. If there was a way to communicate, they did it.

The 1,400-mile distance wasn't ideal, but the couple made it work. Still, they were pining to be with each other.

With about a year left in his military career, Tony was relaxing in his RV with the air conditioner at full blast to combat the heat (it wasn't "Baghdad heat, but it was brutal.) Denise's name flashed across his cell phone screen. He assumed it would be a typical call in which they discussed their days, made some jokes and planned their next in-person meetup.

"I'm ready to come with you. I'm done with this," Denise said before packing up the house and storing everything. Within days, she was living happily with Tony in their RV in the Arizona heat.

"She was the queen of the trailer park," her husband jokes, noting his wife's penchant for meeting people and making them feel at ease. If the trailer park had a mayoral election, Denise would have won in a landslide.

Summer 2015

It was the summer of 2015 when Tony decided to hang it up. He retired from the Army and the Green Berets, and he and Denise moved back home to the East Coast. Life wasn't exactly shaping up how Tony thought, particularly after landing a civilian gig testing out a new parachute the Army was fielding. In theory, the job was a natural segue since he was an accomplished paratrooper, and it was supposed to consist primarily of Tony being out in the field. The reality was that it put him in a cubicle wearing a shirt and tie about 75% of the time. To put it lightly, that is not Tony. The only tie Tony wants to deal with is tie-down straps for hauling things in his truck. He doesn't even like ties in soccer.

Needing to find something new, he took a contract job doing overseas security.

"The best way to describe it, I can't say who or what, but we were protecting US personnel and interests in foreign countries," he says of the secretive work.

Denise, meanwhile, went back to school and was a full-time student at Blue Ridge Community College with an eye on a business degree.

One day, while in one of these "interesting" foreign lands, Tony received a smiling selfie from Denise. To this day, Tony doesn't know why that message was sent, but a new tradition began: Denise sent him a daily selfie. Most of them came from her car while waiting at a stoplight.

Tony's new schedule called for him to be out and among the world for 60 days at a time and then be home for 45 days, which fit his lifestyle just fine. Plus, it allowed him and Denise to take frequent vacations to Cancun, where they would drink margaritas by the beach all day.

The schedule: Wake up. Eat. Drink tequila by the ocean. Nap. Drink tequila by the sea. Eat Dinner. Drink tequila. Rinse. Repeat.

More often than not, the couple traveled with Gary and Michelle Potts, the latter of whom became Denise's best friend in fifth grade (not including Konnor, of course). Thick as thieves, Denise and Michelle did everything together and, despite being polar opposites in many ways, they were one and the same. Michelle was the outgoing one, whereas Denise was more standoffish and introverted. Well, she was then. So close the two were, Denise confided in Michelle for everything: the first time she had sex, the time she took a marijuana hit at a local concert, the struggles and joy and being a military wife, what it meant to be a true friend and even better G-Ma (otherwise known as a grandmother.)

"Nobody could say anything bad about me because Denise was on it," Michelle said, recalling when Denise issued a stern warning to Gary.

"If you hurt her, I will hurt you. Mark my words," Denise told Gary.

Even years later, she would say, "Remember what I told you way back? Well, I will still come after you."

While Denise was somewhat reluctant about Gary in the early days, Michelle felt the same about Tony. In fact, she didn't like him in the beginning. At all.

As the years went on, the ice thawed and all parties grew to adore each other. Michelle and Gary's middle son is even named after Tony. When the men proposed (almost a year apart to the day) Denise and Michelle were delighted to see that they received that exact same engagement ring.

Despite Tony's deployments, the foursome would get together for a vacation every year, oftentimes at exotic, beachside locations. Ironically, Denise wasn't a strong swimmer and was terrified of the ocean, but she treasured the salt-kissed air of resort towns. Once in Cozumel, Mexico, a tiny island off the Caribbean Sea, Denise reluctantly went into the open water with Tony on a paddleboard.

"She sat on the paddle board and let Tony paddle her around, but she was just petrified of the ocean," Michelle said.

More of a land shark, Denise liked to admire the ocean from afar or from the bar, and she never passed up an opportunity to stand up on a bar and blurt out a song, usually 4 Non Blondes' 1993 smash "What's Up." A beer bottle almost always substituted as a microphone, similar to when a little girl uses a hairbrush and sings into a mirror. Comfortable with some liquid courage, sometimes she'd even wander behind the bar and pretend to serve drinks.

In 2016, while planning another vacation, Denise read about a three-day music festival in Las Vegas in the fall called the Route 91 Harvest Festival. It had been going for a few years and everyone seemed to rave about it. That particular year was headlined by Luke Bryan, Brad Paisley and Toby Keith, all prominent singers who dominated the music charts. The undercard was impressive, too: Little Big Town and Chris Young were among them. Both avid country music listeners, Denise told her husband they had to go, and he didn't hesitate.

That year, Tony and Denise stayed near the concert site at the Luxor, the pyramid-shaped hotel that's supposed to emulate Egypt. A faux Nile River used to run through the property. It's perhaps most known for its bright beam that sits atop the pyramid, the most powerful man-made light in the world. Legend says you can see it from space, but most credible reports dismiss that notion. Still, it can be seen from hundreds of miles away on clear nights. In 2009's Up In The Air, George Clooney's character called it a "shit hole," claiming, "nobody stays there."

From where the concert was, the Luxor location couldn't be better. In 2017, though, Tony and Denise opted to rest their heads at Bally's, a central hotel on the Las Vegas Strip that has since been rebranded as the Horseshoe. The land that the Horseshoe sits on is somewhat infamous in Las Vegas, as it was once home to the MGM Grand. That building opened in 1973, and Dean Martin entertained the masses. Things were going swimmingly at the resort until a fire started in a refrigerated pastry display in a casino restaurant called The Deli in 1980. When the fire began, 5,000 people were in the hotel, and flames spread quickly through the ceiling vents. Although the flames were limited to the casino level, smoke and toxic fumes worked their way up shafts and into rooms. In the end, 85 died, most from smoke inhalation and carbon monoxide poisoning. Eventually, the casino was rebuilt and Bally's took over in 1986.

Most Vegas visitors have no idea about the history of that street corner. Hell, a lot of Vegas locals probably don't know either. They probably only know the modern-day MGM Grand that eventually opened south of its original location.

More than 30 years after that fatal fire, Denise was strolling through the controlled chaos of Bally's and sat at a Megabucks slot machine. After slipping a $20 bill into the machine, she pushed the button to spin the reels repeatedly, but she wasn't walking away with any money. There, an unexpected visitor approached her. Denise had never seen this woman before.

"I'm a palm reader in town here, and I don't do this outside of my shop," the stranger divulged, "but I had to stop and tell you that you have an aura coming off of you."

Not knowing what to think about this unsolicited slot machine encounter, Denise exchanged pleasantries with the allegedly in-tune woman, but she was shaken. The brief encounter affected her mentality, and her happy-go-lucky spirit changed. She was reflective and immediately told her husband about the odd conversation.

The next day, around lunchtime, the couple reclined on plastic chairs and absorbed Vitamin D from the sun on the Bally's pool deck. Tony had just snatched up a few drinks from the bustling pool bar and returned to his wife. For reasons unknown, he suddenly blurted out, "If anything ever happens to me, I want you to be happy."

It wasn't the booze talking. He meant it. Truth be told, considering his life of work, he was much more at risk than she.

This nondescript woman, for better or for worse, prompted a longer discussion between the couple of 32 years. For the next hour, they spoke earnestly about the future and the "what ifs" that came with it. They joked throughout the conversation so as not to let the levity of the talk overwhelm them, and Tony felt great peace afterward.

That conversation came that afternoon of Oct. 1, 2017.

Oct. 1, 2017, 5 p.m.

The sun was still high overhead and air conditioning was blasting air hard into Bally's when Tony and Denise strolled to the back of the hotel and hopped on a monorail to ferry them south toward the Route 91 grounds, also called Las Vegas Village.

The day itself was beautiful, and the duo was already planning on returning to the 2018 version of the music festival in Vegas, regardless of the headliners. Next year, they said they would convince Michelle and Gary to come. The prospect of bringing Michelle and Gary wouldn't be difficult, as they were supposed to attend the 2017 festival, too, but the welcoming of a new grandchild kept them in West Virginia.

On the afternoon of Oct. 1, 2017, Michelle's cell rang, and she noticed Denise was FaceTiming her.

"You're coming to Vegas next year, birth or no birth of your grandbaby!" Denise demanded in a jovial tone.

"Yes. We'll be there. I'm really sorry. I wish we were there."

"Shell," Denise continued, using the nickname everyone seemed to know. "This is against my norm, but I'm wearing flip-flops tonight because my boots gave me blisters last night!"

Tony and Denise mainly hung out on the west side of the Village, taking in all the music acts. They even posted a photo to social media that day—another selfie, obviously. In the picture, they radiated happiness. They didn't know it, but they weren't far from where Mary Jo von Tillow stood with her husband, Kurt, and their family. Like Mary Jo, he had no way of knowing that he'd be a widow by evening's end.

Not long before Jason Aldean, the evening's headliner, took that stage, Tony noticed something amiss with his wife.

"You okay?" he wondered, thinking that odd slot machine conversation still gripped her.

"I'm just not feeling it," she said as the three days of music, sun, drinking and all things Las Vegas finally caught up to her.

"Let's go."

"No," Denise contended, "let's stay a little longer."

"You sure?

"I'm sure."

If only they did leave.

Fifteen minutes after choosing to stay, the sound of a few small explosions rang through the Las Vegas village, but then things returned to normal. In an instant, though, all hell broke loose when a volley of bullets came down on the crowd, and Tony and Denise were in the crosshairs.

Oct. 1, 2017, 10:05 p.m.

From his military career, Tony certainly knew what gunshots sounded like, particularly after that day of clearing the village in Iraq, but the sounds of that night somehow didn't register for him. At least not immediately.

"Is that gunfire?" Denise asked her husband as his eyes darted to Mandalay Bay. Not seeing a muzzle flash, Tony deduced that there was nothing to fear. It was probably pyrotechnics, he assumed. Seconds later, a second volley rang out, and Tony's military-trained ear knew that those were indeed gunshots.

Still, many country music fans in the venue weren't reacting, as they seemed to think maybe a speaker had blown. Not Tony and Denise. They were already starting to make their way out of the venue, not knowing they were in the midst of what would become the largest mass shooting incident in United States history. A gunman perched on

Mandalay Bay's 32nd floor with automatic weapons was shooting aimlessly at the crowd, picking off people one by one. The hotel looked directly down at the open-air concert venue that stood on one of the busiest, most famous streets in the country — maybe even the world. The shots were coming down incredibly rapidly due to the fact that the madman was using a bump stock, which essentially makes guns fire faster.

Go, go, go. Run, run, run.

Tony, like so many in that moment, assumed the threat was coming from the ground level, especially after not seeing a muzzle flash from the towering hotel across the street. All the scenarios were racing through his head: Will there be an ambush by the exit? Are there hidden explosives waiting to take us out when we leave? How many gunmen are there?

He held Denise's hand and led her through the 27,000 people, often looking back to make sure she was okay running in her flip-flops. The exit was in sight, about 30 yards from them, when the crowd panicked, finally realizing what was happening. Jason Aldean ran off the stage to seek cover.

Go, go, go. Run, run, run.

Again, while holding her hand, Tony looked back at Denise as they slalomed through the crowd. It was then, while peering back, that he saw the love of his life's upper body thrust forward as a bullet entered the back of her head. Immediately unconscious, Denise collapsed to the asphalt. Tony had seen enough wartime injuries to know what a deadly wound looked like, and he realized that things were dire and probably fatal. This was bad. Really bad.

By now, a third, and seemingly forever, volley of bullets was pouring down on the crowd like a relentless rainstorm, leading Tony to cover his still-breathing wife with his shaking body. For 11 minutes, bullets dotted the crowd, all while Denise fought to stay alive. When would they wake up from this awful nightmare?

As the lights in the venue dimmed, Tony, a realist, knew Denise wouldn't make it, but he never wanted to be wrong so badly in his life.

"The warrior in me left, and I said, 'I'll just let him come take me, too, because I'm not leaving her,'" he recalls.

Lying on the ground, Tony's only thought was getting Denise to an ambulance, but how? Just then, he saw what appeared to be a motorized scooter just over an arm's reach away, and an escape plan was formulated. The flurry of bullets was steady and endless when he crouched down, extended his brawny arm and dragged the scooter toward his wife.

"Please don't take that," a woman's voice suddenly cut through the noise, "that's my only way out of here."

The woman, who was visibly disabled, pleaded with her words and her teary eyes. She was terrified. Her entire existence relied on that mobile ride.

"What the fuck!" Tony screamed into the air as his conscience couldn't let him jack the scooter and leave this woman stranded. Again, he got the asphalt beside his wife.

Sheer chaos unfolded as Tony resisted the urge to lift Denise onto the scooter and ride away. People were running, ducking or taking cover behind anything. For a brief moment, a female police officer joined the duo on the ground, her gun drawn in her right hand. Down on all fours, her eyes trained on the exits while trying to deduce what was happening. Tony's eyes, meanwhile, soon shifted from the exits to her gun, believing gunmen would soon rush in from the southeast gates.

"I can take this fucking pill from her, and I can go fucking stop this right down," he thought as the "warrior" mentality returned.

Once Special Forces, always Special Forces.

Despite legitimately contemplating snatching the gun five to ten times, someone kept him from doing it: Denise. He could not leave her. The police officer eventually got up and ran toward the sound of gunfire, all but eliminating Tony's chance to take matters into his own hands.

This all felt like an eternity, and all he could do was lie with his wife behind two plastic garbage cans until either he was shot or the shooting ended. He honestly wasn't quite sure which ending he wanted, but the latter happened.

What Tony and no one in the venue knew was that police had located the gunman in his 32nd-floor hotel room. A coward, he took his own life before officers could get to him.

Once the venue lights turned back on, the concert crowd had thinned out, and death was all around. Men were taking off their shirts and belts to make tourniquets for the wounded. Aquafina water bottles were used to wash off blood.

A rallying cry of "Help! Somebody, help" echoed.

From the corner of his eye, Tony noticed a man with what had previously been used as a decorative wheelbarrow coming toward him. Finally, he thought, a way to get Denise out of here. With help from others, he gently laid Denise into the yellow tray of the one-wheeled landscaping cart and pushed his wife away from the chaos. Her respiration had slowed way down as Tony continued speaking loudly to her between breaths, and he began tilting the wheelbarrow to try to open up her airway better.

"I know you can hear me. Babe, you gotta fight hard."

Having escaped out the east side of the venue, Tony searched high and low for an ambulance, but none appeared. People were literally running for their lives all around him. It wasn't entirely as if Marshall Law had been declared, but little rhyme or reason was happening. Terrified concertgoers were justifiably panicked, as many jumped over fences or even tried to get into cars they didn't own.

Many shooting victims were being taken out in wheelbarrows or wheelchairs, carried out on security gates or slung over a friend's shoulder. With Denise clinging to life, two women in a blue 1994 Ford Ranger pulled right up to Tony. He didn't know who they were.

"Put her in the bed of the truck and get in. We'll get you to a hospital," the driver, a woman named Sue Ann Cornwell with a gray mullet, said. Another woman sat in the passenger seat.

Because of the unanticipated mass casualty event, ambulance services were already largely exhausted, so this woman's transportation services seemed like a decent option in a bad situation. It was maybe the only option. He had nothing to lose by getting into the back of a truck driven by a woman he'd never met or seen. A third woman who had only recently graduated from nursing school also jumped into the pickup bed.

Sue Ann floored it. A speeding ticket was the least of her concerns, nor would she have stopped had a cop attempted to pull her over.

Tony's feet were dangling off the tailgate when Sue Ann took off, whizzing through the streets of Vegas at breakneck speeds. As she raced down the roads, Tony could hear Sue Ann screaming at other cars to "move" and "get out of the way" through the truck's sliding back window. Ironically, some of the roads Sue Ann took that night were just blocks from what would later become the track for the Las Vegas Formula One Grand Prix race. Sue Ann could have qualified for the race at the rate she was going on Oct. 1, 2017.

As the crisp air sped by, Tony hugged his wife and checked for a heartbeat throughout the entire drive on the city streets and Interstates 15 and 215, two of the city's main arteries.

"You gotta hang on!" he kept pleading from the bed of the truck.

Denise hung on as long as she could, but her pulse ground to a halt and stopped before they could make it to the hospital.

While his warrior spirit left him in a parking lot 30 minutes prior, his heart and soul left him in the back of a 1994 Ford Ranger on a Vegas freeway. Looking at the nursing student who was closer to the truck's open cabin window, Tony uttered words he never wanted to say.

"You can tell them that we can stop now," he said, as Sue Ann flew down the freeway at speeds well over the posted limit. "We don't have to go 90."

The urgency was gone. So was Denise. Like Tony, the nurse checked for a pulse and found none. Although Denise was officially declared dead at the hospital, she literally died in Tony's arms on the freeway.

Lost and speechless, Tony mourned as the truck got caught in a bumper-to-bumper traffic jam. With nowhere to go, Sue Ann got out of the driver's seat, opened the door of the truck, hopped out, walked two feet and cracked open the lid to a truck-mounted toolbox in the bed of the truck. Reaching in with her right hand, she pulled out a blanket and handed it to Tony — it was a small act, but something appreciated.

"Let's give her some respect," Sue Ann sadly said, referring to the woman she had never met but who took her last breath in the back of her truck.

Getting under the cover and still holding Denise's body, Tony sobbed and repeated: "Can she hear me? Can she hear me?"

Eventually, a local police officer was made aware of the situation and led the truck to the Spring Valley Hospital Medical Center's emergency room doors.

At a loss for words and crocodile tears streaming down his face, Tony simply said, "Thank you" as the women in the truck drove away.

The hospital staff was ready. Denise was put on a gurney and wheeled into a small room inside the facility, which is nestled nicely in southwest Vegas. The hospital is well regarded for its maternity services, an irony as Denise officially lost her life there.

As the unrealistic reality again set in, Tony spent a few minutes with his deceased wife underneath the fluorescent lights of a medical center. A generic, 300-thread count white sheet had been placed over her, which he gently pulled down at least 10 times to take a look.

"Maybe I got the wrong person?" he wondered.

Unfortunately, the face looking back at him every time was Denise's. She was one of 58 people to die that evening.

As he'd been tending to his wife and paying no attention to news bulletins, Tony still didn't know who did this to Denise. He assumed it was a terrorist group. Sadness was replaced by retribution.

"I swore vengeance at that time. No matter how big of a fucking cell network it was, I was going to fucking do them in, and I swore vengeance at that time. I was going to do that," he recalls.

A TV in the corner of the waiting room was turned on to a local channel, which was reporting on the shooting. While sitting there, Tony glanced up at the TV and was able to assess the scope of the situation. At the time, the number of dead wasn't confirmed, but it was growing (Denise's death had yet to be included in the count.) During that same news report, though, it was confirmed that the gunman committed suicide in his adjoining hotel rooms, suites 32-135 and 32-134, as police were closing in.

In a flash, Tony lost not only his wife but also the man he fully intended to hunt down and kill.

Oct. 2, 2017

Like Mary Jo and so many others who lost loved ones on Oct. 1, 2017, Tony didn't know what to do. His wife was gone, and he was now alone in Las Vegas, nearly 2,400 miles from home… the home he shared with his now-deceased wife. All of her things were still there, all the things she planned on coming home to. Like many brand-new widows, Tony vowed not to leave Vegas without his partner and planned to stay in the city until Denise's body was released.

Around 5 a.m., he realized there was nothing more he could do at Spring Valley Hospital, so the medical staff ordered an Uber to get him back to Bally's. The cold chill that began the night before was still hovering as he went outside to wait in the darkness. The morning sun was yet to rise as he stood in stunned silence, looking at the sleeping homes and businesses surrounding the hospital.

A sedan slowed, only for the driver to find Tony covered in blood and wrapped in a hospital sheet.

His Uber had arrived.

"Dude," the shocked driver said in a hushed tone. Nothing more needed to be said, and nothing else was said.

Wrapped in his hospital-acquired blanket and looking very much worse for wear, Tony walked into Bally's as a widower. There, while still swaddled in the bloody blanket, he walked to the front desk to extend his stay. He then headed to his now lonely room.

Swinging open the door, he was greeted by his wife's open suitcase, which rested atop a luggage rack full of shirts and "fancy pants." Her cowboy boots settled on the floor, and her toiletries and makeup were still perfectly laid out near the bathroom sink. Denise wasn't forgotten, but these were reminders that she wasn't there.

Playing Monday morning quarterback, Tony wondered, "What could I have done differently?"

He had already contacted family and close friends and told them the news — Mallorie even hung up on him because she didn't believe what she was hearing — but his phone had been blowing up all morning.

"Are you two ok????" one person asked in a text message. Well over 30 messages carried that same sentiment. He responded to almost none of them, instead penning a message on Facebook to confirm the worst.

"It saddens me to say that I lost my wife of 32 years, a mother of two, soon to be grandmother of five this evening in the Las Vegas shooting," he wrote. "Denise passed in my arms. I LOVE YOU BABE."

Tony, a very tactical man in his life, was a shell of his former self. He scrolled through old photos of Denise and went through every emotion you could think of —almost like he had emotional schizophrenia. He has little memory of how Oct. 2 played out, but he remembers a sympathetic hotel security officer coming to check on him.

Oct. 3, 2017

About 36 hours after losing his wife, Tony wasn't close to picking up the pieces of his life, but wanted to pick up a piece of Denise, her purse, which was left behind during the disarray. With the city wrapped in sorrow, Tony demurely walked the nearly two miles from Bally's to the shooting site, getting as close as officers would let him.

"My wife was shot the other night, and her purse is in there."

A Las Vegas Metro police officer forbade Tony from going further. The festival grounds were an active crime scene.

Not only was the south end of Las Vegas Boulevard flush with police officers and crime scene investigators, but hordes of media were present. For reasons he doesn't know, Tony did several media interviews, including one with CNN's Anderson Cooper.

"In 32 years, he grew stronger every day. It just got better every day," he said with remarkable poise, particularly given that a busted-out window of Mandalay Bay directly to his left served as a heartbreaking reminder of what happened. A photo of Tony and Denise with three or their grandkids flashed on the screen, showing them at Disney World.

His purse objective unsuccessful, Tony headed the 1.9 miles back toward his hotel on foot. While walking the somber Strip, he strolled past his hotel and ended up on the sidewalk in front of the Flamingo Hotel. He stopped to gaze at Caesars Palace and looked up into the blue sky. A Southwest Airlines plane was heading West somewhere. His face looking upward, he heard cars driving by and the faint sound of slot machines singing, but something else caught his attention, something familiar. Lowering his head, he stood there slowly, pacing and looking toward the sound, which was getting louder. Two women, probably in their early 30s, casually walked by, arm in arm. Their eyes glistened and their mouths moved while they loudly and merrily sang a song older than them. The song: "Don't Stop Believing."

That was Denise's song. She was always singing that damn song.

Tony froze, and his eyes widened. He smiled and wanted to tell the girls about his wife and her love of that Journey song, but he couldn't. He lost it and started crying hysterically on the sidewalk.

"There's a reason I was walking there at that particular moment," he says.

Denise was already sending him signs.

Dozens of people reached out to Tony and offered to help, but there were two women he really wanted to see: the women who drove Denise to the hospital in the truck. It wasn't lost on Tony that these women were put through their own kind of trauma, but he had no idea where to find them. He didn't even remember getting their names.

Returning to his hotel room with that damn Journey song stuck in his head, Tony crumbled on the floor, leaned against the wall and began wading through hundreds of Facebook condolences. A message pinged.

"I am the one that drove the truck trying to get Denise help. I want you to know my heart is broken. We did all we could. You are an awesome husband," the message read.

It was from Sue Ann and her sister, Billie Jo LaCount.

Oct. 5, 2017

Wearing pensive smiles, Sue Ann and Billie Jo walked in the door of Bally's and officially met the man whom they last saw holding his deceased wife in the back of a Ford Ranger.

During that meeting, Tony learned about Sue Ann, a retired bus driver in Vegas. Billie Jo had been visiting from Wisconsin. He also got to tell the women all about his wife.

"She was the backbone of our family," he said during that meeting and spoke about their four grandkids, a fifth on the way. The grandkids, who called Denise "G-Ma," were the light of her life.

Not a dry eye among them, he told the women of the vacations they went on and about their many RV and camping trips. He relayed that Denise wanted to pursue sports and nutrition after graduating from college, and she also considered starting a nonprofit to support military veterans.

His fist clenched and covered his mouth. He added, "She was always so happy," which led him to describe her passion for sending him daily selfies, which he looked forward to every day. She even coached her husband on how to take a proper selfie.

It had been two days since he got a selfie from Denise, and he wouldn't be getting them anytime soon.

For three weeks, Mallorie didn't leave her brother's couch. She was mourning and in a bit of a blackout state, but she was also pregnant with her second son. Seeing as she didn't want to speak to anyone, being a recluse suited her just fine as her mother's death became the talk of the small Martinsburg town.

A children-focused thrift store offered free clothes for Denise's grandkids. The local Dairy Queen's marquee read

"Rest in Peace, Denise" in the days following the shooting. At Hedgesville High School, where Tony and Denise fell in love, 300 people attended a candlelight vigil on the football field. Photos were displayed on the field's scoreboard, many of them selfies. Tony didn't attend, as he was still in Vegas making arrangements to get Denise's body home, but a livestream camera was set up in the bleachers so he could watch from his hotel room, which he did.

"Knowing the person Denise was, she would say to you, 'Don't quit, don't get bitter, don't get angry. Don't let the other side win,'" Pastor Tom Snyder told the crowd. The Hedgesville football team honored Denise all season, wearing a helmet sticker of her initials below the blue and gold Eagles mascot.

Lying on that couch, which amounted to her three-week home, Mallorie couldn't stop thinking about a fun, casual conversation with her mom. In late September, just one week before Vegas, she went to an ultrasound appointment and found out her unborn child was a boy.

"Please name him Grayson. I love that name. Name him Grayson," Denise pleaded. "I'll throw it in the hat for you, mom," Mallorie said while rolling her eyes.

That conversation played in Mallorie's head over and over — "Please name him Grayson." "I love that name."

In February 2018, Mallorie welcomed a boy. His name is Grayson.

Mom won again.

Tony took several years off work to face a new life without his wife by his side. A GoFundMe set up by a friend helped, as did money that came via a legal settlement with MGM International, the owner of Mandalay Bay. He was also obviously getting money from the military for his years of service.

He soon started posting selfies of Denise on his social media to keep her memory alive, pictures he'd received over the years.

Not long after returning home to West Virginia, his cell phone pinged. It was a smiling selfie from Sue Ann, gray mullet and all. Not long after, Billie Jo sent him a selfie.

"We call it the Selfie Movement," Sue Ann told the Las Vegas Review-Journal.

Largely invested in Tony and Denise's love story, Sue Ann now takes care of Denise's dedicated area at the Healing Garden in Las Vegas, where the 58 are permanently honored. Her truck, that same 1994 Ford Ranger, bears a "Route 91 Festival" bumper sticker. Next to them are stickers of angel wings and the name Denise Salmon Burditus. Although she never met Denise, Sue Ann considers her family.

Denise's memorial at the Healing Garden sits about four spots away from the spot dedicated to Mary Jo's husband. It's somewhat fitting since they stood near each other at the Route 91 concert on Oct. 1, 2017, albeit unknowingly.

Mary Jo had never known Tony before that evening, but they met at the Country Music Awards in Nashville a month later when the 58 victims were honored. There, Carrie Underwood sang the Christian hymn "Softly and Tenderly" as pictures of the 58 scrolled on a screen behind her.

Having settled into his new routine, Tony is back to work and tapping into his roots. He teaches evasive driving, handgun training, range training, firearms training and some off-road training.

Unlike some who lost family on Route 91, Tony never blamed Vegas for what happened. He's gone back many times, saying he's going to have fun as a way to honor his always-smiling wife.

"We want to make sure her memory lives on, but not by how she died — because she was so much more than that," Denise's daughter-in-law, Christina Burditus, told The Cullman Times in Alabama, where she and Joshua Burditus live. "We do not want to have the emphasis placed on how Denise died. There was just so much more to her. I hope that, by sharing her story, it is in honor of her life."

Although he was initially very guarded, Mary Jo has gotten to know Tony quite well since that night, and they even met up in Vegas just a couple of months later to return to the venue. Creating boundaries — at least then — they didn't go inside the fenced-off location that claimed their loved ones, but instead stood outside the gates and looked through.

Gone was the mess of torn shirts, hats, cups and debris that coated the ground when they were last there. Gone was the yellow "do not cross" tape that previously wrapped the fencing. Some of the area seemed frozen in time, as part of the stage was still erected, giving off a ghostly feeling. A semi-truck trailer remained. Memorials and flowers were still pinned to the fence and on the ground.

Mary Jo and Tony's stories were surprisingly similar, as they both have kids around the same ages; they both have grandkids; Tony and Denise were married 32 years, whereas Kurt and Mary Jo were married 34 years.

They've become awfully close via an awful circumstance. Tony has even gotten close with Tommy Maher, too, and they've gone out on Honor Trips together. The trio of Tony, Mary Jo and Tommy went to Virginia Beach after a shooting there in 2019. Coincidentally enough, Tony's West Virginia community now raises money via an annual kickball tournament, and the money actually supports Tommy's good deeds.

"Tony shares with me much more than he shares with others," Mary Jo says.

It's a traumatic bond that, thankfully, few will ever understand. Michelle Potts even sees a lot of Denise in Mary Jo.

"It's kind of scary," Michelle opined, claiming that their mannerisms are similar, as is how the women carry themselves.

"I obviously have no baseline for comparison," Mary Jo notes, adding, "Tony makes me feel safe."

Michelle and Gary honor Denise yearly by doing random acts of kindness on Denise's birthday, June 5. A fitness instructor, Michelle always gives away free classes to her gym members on Oct. 1, too. She and Gary have taken free meals to first responders, and they often pay for strangers' meals at restaurants.

"I feel like hate took her, but I want everyone to know that love wins. Even though we lost her, we're gaining love by spreading it," Michelle says.

Once the strong, silent type, Tony now wears his emotions on his sleeve. He thinks about his wife daily and tries to honor her with happiness, even if it means listening to Journey now and again. While he isn't actively looking for signs from his late wife, he admits she might be signaling to him occasionally, similar to those two women singing "Don't Stop Believing" on the Vegas Strip.

"A sign from Denise is gonna have to slap me in the fucking face. I don't see things and think, 'Oh, that's a sign,'" he said.

But there was one undeniable sign six years after Denise's death, however, and it happened on her birthday.

On June 5, 2023, Tony took his grandson Kane to a football camp being put on by West Virginia University. Chalk it up to grandfather duties. While sitting in the stands, Tony proudly peered down and saw Kane on the grass. He looked so small out there amid the 100-yard field. Huddled up with other kids at the camp, Tony leaned in when he noticed the number his grandson was wearing on his football jersey. It was the number 58 — the same number of people who were killed in Las Vegas that night. Denise was one of the 58.

Like he did in his hotel room while looking at pictures of Denise, Tony was at a loss for words. He kept tilting his head, squinting and doing double-takes to ensure that his eyes weren't deceiving him, but every time he looked, Kane's jersey number was 58. Feelings of happiness, sadness and shock took over. He couldn't believe this was real, especially since it was Denise's birthday.

Once the football camp ended, Tony stood up from his seat and went to the field to congratulate his grandson. They hugged, and Grandad spoke of the pride he felt for Kane, but there was one thing he had to know. It was eating away at him as they left the football stadium. While walking to his nearby truck parked under the overcast sky, Tony couldn't help himself. He needed to ask his grandson a question.

"Did you pick that number?"

"No," Kane shrugged, "they just gave it to me."

There it was. That was his sign. It slapped him across the fucking face.

CHAPTER 7

Ronald Benjamin

January 2023

"It metastasized to your liver. You have Stage 4 cancer."

After hearing those words, Ronald Benjamin, flanked by his wife, Amy, stared blankly at the colon surgeon. The notion of having an aggressive form of cancer was never something he thought about.

Just a few weeks earlier, Ron underwent a routine colonoscopy at a Beverly, Massachusetts, medical center.

"I'm not worried about it," he had joked to a friend before the everyday procedure. "I'm Italian. We die of heart attacks."

High blood pressure is a common theme in Ron's life, as is early death. His great-grandfather died at the age of 54. His grandfather died after turning 60. Now, here was Ron at 51, receiving news that his life was hanging in the balance. He knew the colonoscopy results didn't come back clean after being told that some troublesome polyps were found, but this was not the news he expected to hear.

The energy drained from his body, from the top of his head to his feet, as his health status was absorbed. Although sitting on a chair with a window over his shoulder showing off the beautiful Boston suburbs, Ron couldn't walk. He couldn't even stand up. Every muscle was tingling and locked up. His jaw was on the floor.

"Do you mind if I just sit here for a while?"

"Take as much time as you need."

July 2005

Ron was cranky and exhausted when the woman of his dreams came into his life.

The day before, he and a pal had driven two-and-a-half hours from northeast Massachusetts to Mashantucket, Conn., to gamble at Foxwoods, the largest resort casino in North America. Following a marathon all-nighter at the blackjack and craps tables amid the 9,000,000 square-foot resort, the two decided it was time to cash in and begin their boring, two-and-a-half-hour drive back home via Interstate 395.

He'd just gotten home and hadn't even taken off his shoes when he got a call from a friend prodding him to meet at a local bar.

"Dude, I just drove two-and-a-half hours there, two-and-a-half hours back. I've been up for 24 hours gambling, and I'm tired."

"Come for a drink."

Whether it was FOMO, a second wind or not wanting to get harassed for being "lame," Ronnie made the quick jaunt to the bar and met his pal, Brian, on the bar's second floor. A cold beer in hand, Ron lamented being there when his bed was just a few miles away. The night was growing darker and darker as the minutes ticked by.

Although his eyes were bloodshot from sleep deprivation, they soon widened when a brunette knockout started walking toward him. The woman, it seemed, knew Brian and spoke to him congenially. Noticing the man with Brian, she stuck out her hand.

"I'm Amy," she said. Rather than immediately extending his arm as a courtesy, Ronnie just looked at her hand curiously. Ron's hesitancy didn't last long, but it lasted long enough for Amy to think, "This guy is a grump!"

Granted, Ron eventually placed his palm in hers to reciprocate the gesture, but his first impression wasn't impressive.

Three weeks passed, and neither Ronnie nor Amy thought much about that night or their brief meeting. He thought she was beautiful but unavailable, and she thought he was cute but uninterested.

On a cold, rainy day, Ron headed to the Market Basket grocery store for some goods. A fixture in New England, the family-owned store has approximately 90 locations and is recognized for its affordable, high-quality products and employee-friendly work environment. It's almost always ranked among the best supermarkets in the country.

Holding a basket full of fresh vegetables and various condiments, Ron was nearing the end of his grocery store pit stop when he looked down the aisle and saw a recognizable face. This time, he smiled while approaching the woman he'd met at the bar through their mutual friend.

Surrounded by fresh-baked bread, tubs of mayonnaise and frozen fish sticks, the two really began speaking for the first time. He discovered that Amy was a traveling nurse, and she learned he was a machinist; they both spoke of their love for Boston sports, especially the Red Sox, who were just coming off their first World Series win in 86 years after vanquishing the hated New York Yankees and St. Louis Cardinals.

Unlike the bar, their grocery store meeting was unforgettable, and Ronnie wanted to see her again. He had never met anyone like her: she was intelligent, stunning, driven and independent. He thought about their conversation several times over a couple of days. It wasn't that Amy was living full-time in his mind, per se, but she at least had an Airbnb up there.

Unsure of how to break the ice, he grabbed his phone and dialed her number, which went to voicemail. Shit, he had to quickly think of something coherent, and the words just started coming out.

"Hey, it's Ron. We met at the grocery store the other day. I was going shopping and I was wondering if maybe you might give me a call and help me out with my shopping list."

Was the pickup line borderline pathetic? Maybe. But believe it or not, it worked, and the two began living together within a month.

January 2023

The ride home from the hospital wasn't long — less than 15 minutes with traffic. Collecting his thoughts, Ron decided to let his large Italian family know, but he wanted to keep his health secret from his three teenage sons, not wanting them to think their dad's life had an expiration date. But, following a lengthy discussion, Ron and Amy decided to tell the boys in an age-appropriate and optimistic way, focusing on the excellent doctors helping their dad feel better.

"There will be times when daddy is really tired and not going to feel so great, and sometimes the way he looks might change a little bit too," Amy explained in the living room, trying to keep the mood light but also serious. "If you see dad not looking so great or not feeling so great, it's part of the process. Dad's gonna have good days and bad days, and you're entitled to that, too."

As expected, the boys absorbed all the information they were receiving about their dad's health. They were probably even more resilient than their parents gave them credit for.

"Ok, well, I got this. Can I be excused?" Ryan, the couple's middle son, who's high-functioning autistic, asked.

"Sure."

For the next few minutes, mom and dad continued to field questions and carefully consider their answers when

Ryan reappeared in the living room with a plastic Poland Springs water bottle in his hand. The color wasn't clear, but somewhat opaque with bits of toilet paper floating.

The words "Cancer Fighting Potion" were written on the bottle.

"Dad," the tyke said, handing Ronnie the bottle. "I mixed this up for you, and this potion is going to help you fight your cancer."

"Thanks, bud," Ron, smiling his mouth, eyes and heart, said, "this is probably what I needed."

To this day, no one knows what's in the bottle, nor did Ronnie drink it, but he would often tell a very proud Ryan that the potion "was working."

The bottle now sits up high in a kitchen cupboard alongside snacks hidden from the kids.

With the family aware of the health battle that lay ahead of Ronnie, the weeks went by in a blur, and one oncologist even told him to get his affairs in order. Still, Ronnie felt fine and continued his work as a machinist at Benco Precision Machining, a Gloucester, Mass., company he purchased from his parents in 2000. The Big C, however, hovered over everything. He questioned whether to attend certain things, like a friend's celebration of life, and focused on ensuring he tied up loose ends if things went south in a hurry.

Following four rounds of chemotherapy, where fluids were pumped into his veins via a chest port for three to four hours at a time, Ronnie wondered if it was all for naught.

Returning home from work one evening, Ronnie sat on the second stair of his home and began taking off his boots, which were always covered in metallic dust and shimmering shavings.

The door to the home swung open, jarring him. It was Amy.

"65%," she said through a steady stream of tears.

Mentally and physically exhausted from his workday, which consisted of him thinking constantly about cancer, Ron shook his head.

"Babe, you can't do this to me right now," he said. "I understand you're upset, but you can't do this to me right now. Walk out the door, calm down."

"65%," she repeated.

"What are you talking about?"

"Ronnie, your cancer shrank 65%."

She could barely get the words out of her mouth amid the grateful sobbing.

Tears immediately gushed out of Ron's eyes as he was full of emotion. He had been thinking his cancer would shrink 6%, maybe 12% if he were being overly optimistic.

The exhaustion of the day was replaced by faith and hope, but it was short-lived after the oncologist, the same one who advised Ron to get his affairs in order, told him to stay the course and refused even to consider removing the cancer or burning it out. The oncologist was already on thin ice with Ron and Amy, as he was 45 minutes late for their first appointment because he chose to make a coffee run for his wife. In a follow-up appointment, he took a call from his daughter to help her figure out an iPad passcode. Ron, meanwhile, was in a life-and-death situation.

Frustrated, he grabbed Amy's hand.

"We're out of here."

As this played out and the family sought out answers, a woman Ron had never met heard his story and reached out on social media. In a message, she said, "My mother is friends with your aunt and uncle. I went through the same thing you did. You need to go see Dr. Qadan at Mass General."

Ron was desperate and took any advice. If someone had told him to eat leaves from a maple tree, he'd happily munch on sap. If someone told him to bathe in cat urine, he'd get the tub ready. No, he never did these things, but you get the idea.

He told Amy about the social media message, and, being a nurse, she delved deep into the doctor's qualifications.

Meeting Motaz Qadan was a breath of fresh air.

"Tell me something about you," he began their conversation.

Every other doctor wanted to know about the cancer, the treatments, or the T-cell count and seemed to identify Ron not by his name but by his disease, so the couple was puzzled by Dr. Qadan's question since they weren't used to being treated like human beings. Until now, no medical professional had ever made the couple feel like we were people with feelings, fears, concerns and despair. So much despair.

Amy, who wears her heart on her sleeve, broke down. This doctor, she thought, was the first step in saving her husband's life.

Unlike the terrible oncologist, Dr. Qadan laid out the options, one of which was a live liver transplant.

"That's a last-case scenario and way out there," the good doc said. "We're so far away from that right now."

Ron broke down. Finally, someone was providing him with solutions. It was the first time he'd ever cried before a man he didn't know.

Following that meeting, Ron went through more chemo, and part of his colon was removed.

"Amy, at least I'll be less of an asshole now," he joked.

Four more rounds of chemo followed, and everything was working, that is, until 11 micro dots of cancer were seen on Ron's liver, where his cancer had metastasized, which was a huge setback.

Again, despair set in. They had done everything right; everything was such precise detail, and now this.

Ron and Amy went over all the options, but he could no longer undergo one proven life-saving procedure that had been previously discussed due to the innumerable tumors throughout his liver. It soon became apparent that a live liver donation, that "last-case scenario" Dr. Qadan had mentioned, was Ron's last and only chance to stay alive. Finding a donor, however, would be difficult and forced Ronnie to change his mindset a bit.

Never wanting to be a burden, Ronnie suddenly found himself asking for help instead of helping, which he's so good at.

"He does the right thing no matter who's looking," Amy beams.

In 2015, the local elementary school held a bake sale to raise money so students could rent a theater and watch the animated comedy Minions. However, the funds came in quite short, and volunteers, including Amy, were defeated. However, the tone shifted after it was determined that they actually did have enough.

As adults hugged and congratulated each other, a woman approached Amy.

"Thank you to you and your husband. What you did just made such a difference to all of these kids here that we're looking forward to this," the woman said.

Curiously, Amy walked up to her husband.

"Is there something you have to tell me?"

"No."

"Why is everybody thanking me?"

"Maybe they really liked the stuff you baked."

"Ronnie," she protested, "why is everybody thanking me? Did you do something?"

Amy knew the answer because he'd done things like this before. Ronnie had opened up his checkbook and made up the deficit.

"I'm a little upset," he confessed while away from all the other rejoining adults, "because I didn't want anyone to know, and I was very, very specific that I didn't want anyone to know."

Turns out that the person in charge spoke of Ron's generosity to just one person, but that person blabbed it to everyone.

"I didn't do it because I wanted people to know I did it. I did it because I saw how hard you guys all worked to make this happen," Ron said nonchalantly.

In a similar fashion, he purchased two new air conditioning units for his elderly grandmother after hers were shot to hell. "They were giving them away for free," he told Granny. She was obviously skeptical of his story — nothing in life is free! — but he never wavered.

He even bought his mother-in-law an enormous TV so she could watch her Telenovelas (Spanish soap operas) on it. Mamacita, as Ron called her, would gush about her son-in-law and show off her TV to friends as if she were modeling it for The Price Is Right.

When Mamacita passed in 2014, Ron took a moment alone with her and even hilariously confessed a secret to her: while in college, he was arrested in Antigua for smoking marijuana.

"I felt guilty keeping that from her all these years," he laughed to his wife.

Amy was adamant that the world could not lose Ronnie's soul, heart or humor. With her husband's health at the forefront of her mind, she made flyers and had a webpage created to bring attention to his battle.

"Hi! I'm Ronnie, and I have stage 4 colon cancer. Due to the extent of cancer in my liver, my only chance at survival is a liver transplant," the website said next to a smiling picture of Ron. "I want nothing more than to grow old with my family, but can't do it without your help."

A few qualifying factors were listed below the message, such as height and blood type.

Ron's health was no longer a secret in Beverly, where he lived, or in the fishing town of Gloucester, where he worked (the same town where much of "The Perfect Storm" was filmed). Family members and strangers stepped forward to help Ron, and many sought to become his donor, but things didn't work out for various reasons.

Ron was back to square one, and time was ticking. Time was his enemy.

December 4, 2020

During the height of the COVID pandemic in 2020, Jessica had had enough: enough of being cooped up in her house, the closed businesses and the facial coverings. It was December, and she had already had enough of the cold winter getting its grip on Connecticut, where she lived.

Relatively new to a divorce, she decided to take a girls' trip to Florida, which was arguably business as usual. Most states had some semblance of a lockdown or stiff restrictions, but Florida was open and full of like-minded people with COVID fatigue.

After coaxing her friend and cousin to join her, the women, all in their 30s, touched down in West Palm Beach, a picturesque, high-society city that sits an hour north of Miami but far less touristy and much more relaxed. One of the most expensive places to live in Florida, West Palm Beach sits on the east side of the phallic-looking state and boasts a diverse population and a cultural hodgepodge of museums, performing arts centers and spring training baseball complexes. Neighboring Palm Beach is home to the 62,500 square foot, 126-room Mar-a-Lago Club, where Donald Trump makes his permanent residence, and Billionaires Row, a stretch of ultra-exclusive, highly valuable waterfront properties.

Florida was the exact opposite of wintery Connecticut. It was warm, and people were aplenty. For many tourists, it was the first time they'd been out of their homes for months, no longer in COVID-aided lockdowns, so they were making up for lost time and letting loose, Jessica and her girls included.

Like moths to a flame, guys were drawn to the three women as they relaxed on the sandy beaches and explored the South Florida cuisine. Still, Jessica wasn't interested in romance, especially anything long-term, given that she was newly split from her husband and in the midst of the divorce. She had a "five-year plan."

"Maybe you'll meet a cute guy," her friend Jen said as they geared up for the trip.

"Oh lord."

"What? You don't know."

"Do not set me up with anyone for five years," Jessica told Jen, repeating what she often told her squad. A one-night stand in Florida, on the other hand, might not be out of the question, but that certainly wasn't her focus.

Still, given the COVID-19 pandemic, some restrictions were evident, particularly at the Two Drunken Goats bar, a relatively weathered beach-themed cantina on Singer Island, situated in a plaza next to a USPS store and a Subway. A sizeable faux tree decorated with clear Christmas lights, oversized ornaments and small goats serves as a centerpiece of the restaurant.

On this day, Dec. 4, the restaurant was trying to keep patrons socially distanced, encouraging them to order drinks inside but retreat to the parking lot or an adjacent breezeway to imbibe. Tall cocktail tables were placed outside, and a DJ set up a makeshift home base on a cobblestone thoroughfare under the stars.

When they got to the bar, Jessica and her friend, Jen, were coming off a long day of Fireball shots and Coors Lights. The third member of their crew, Araina, was hotel-bound, choosing to call it a night rather than keep the party going.

"Ladies, do you two need anything?" a man wearing a belt buckle the size of a small planet asked them almost immediately after arriving.

"No thanks, we're ok."

Taking his cue following the rejection, the women watched him stroll into the restroom. They assumed he must have worked there and applauded his impeccable customer service.

A few moments later, the man returned and asked their drink preference again, making Jessica even more confused about the situation.

"Do you work here?" she demanded.

"No," he laughed. "I'm John. What are your names?"

"So, you don't work here?"

During a brief conversation, John was funny and pleasant and didn't seem like a creep, which was already a selling point. He implored the women to join him and a friend at their outside table, which he motioned toward, but the women saw no friend and were rightfully hesitant. Amicable as ever, however, John sold his vision for the evening, and "the J's" — John, Jessica and Jen — all meandered over to a table to meet another man, who stood up and smiled as the women approached.

This man was handsome and athletic. His short hair fluttered in the slight breeze coming off the Atlantic Ocean.

"I'm Tim," he said, shaking their hands, a real no-no during COVID, as fist bumps were strongly suggested. His half-full Tito's and soda sat on the table; condensation had already formed on the outside of the plastic cup and trickled down to the table, leaving a water ring.

The foursome discovered they were all from the Northeast, but the guys soon realized that despite her ear-to-ear smile, Jessica was there with a heavy heart.

"Today is my dad's birthday," she revealed, "so we're here celebrating. He would have been 59 today."

Keeping details of his death close to the vest, she only revealed that he had passed several years prior.

"So," she continued, "we're here to celebrate him and get away from COVID."

Tim and Jessica hit it off quickly, and he explained that he and his pals were there for a golf trip. They'd gotten a hell of a deal at The Ritz-Carlton Residences, the fanciest hotel in the area, so they couldn't pass up a trip down south. Their three-bedroom penthouse was flush with expensive artwork and ridiculously high-end amenities. A 50-foot wraparound balcony offered them unencumbered views of the glistening skyline.

Like Jessica, Tim was tired of the pandemic-era restrictions and wanted to clear his head. Plus, again, like Jessica, he had two kids. He was also in the midst of a divorce.

"My ex is actually moving out today," he told Jess.

"What do you think you're going to go home to?"

"I have no idea, maybe nothing."

Feeling a kindred spirit of sorts, Jessica told Tim that she, too, was going through a divorce.

"Give me your number," he bravely said, "and we can help each other through this shit."

"You don't want my number."

"I really do."

Tim was unrelenting for the rest of the night before Jessica finally agreed to give him her digits, but she was also pretty confident she'd never see this guy again.

"I'm going to text you. If this is a fake number, I'm going to be so sad."

"It's real."

It was real, both the number and the connection. The next day, Tim and Jessica texted back and forth as he lit it up on the golf course, shooting even-par (hungover, no less!)

"We should all hang out again tonight," he digitally penned after throttling a ball 255 yards down the fairway.

"We're in," she typed back while lying under the sun and absorbing Vitamin D.

Less than 24 hours after meeting in the parking lot-turned-bar, Jessica and Tim were again together, this time at a steakhouse strip club, which is exactly what it sounds like.

Rachel's, ironically a 5-star restaurant, was quite the experience. Jessica had never been to a strip club up to that point, but this wasn't what she imagined. Oiled-up strippers grinded on lubricated silver poles in search of $1 bills as she perused a menu of filet mignon, tomato bruschetta, escargot and caviar.

"You can enjoy your meal inside our elegant dining room or in the middle of the strip club action," Rachel's boasts on its website, claiming it "rivals some of the finest steak houses in the world."

Sitting there with an eyeful of breasts and thongs and an earful of post-grunge rock music, Jessica was tense. Again, Tim made her feel at ease, often joking about the experience.

"Leave it to me to bring you here," he chuckled.

Like Taylor Swift says, "Florida, it's one hell of a drug."

Although she didn't let on at the time, Tim intrigued Jessica. They had similar situations and mindsets. Really, Tim, with all these genuine qualities, reminded her somewhat of her late father, and she'd also met him on her dad's birthday, which she didn't believe was a coincidence. Not long after, Tim learned the circumstances of her father's death, which left him shocked. Respecting her privacy, he didn't pry much, but she discovered that Tim's brother-in-law, also named Tim, passed a year and a half prior, so, like Jessica, he was also mourning the loss of a family member.

Somehow, their planets kept aligning.

Following a whirlwind few days in the Florida sunshine, Jessica and Tim parted and decided to stay in touch without commitments. Perhaps their meeting was a fleeting moment in time, nothing more — a story to tell their friends. Two weeks later, however, Jessica found herself traveling to Massachusetts to meet up with Tim again.

They've been together ever since and have become part of each other's families. Tim became the missing piece in Jessica's complex life.

In other words, that "five-year plan" she was so adamant about didn't turn out as she expected. It turned out better.

Tim Reynolds grew up in Beverly, Mass., where Ronald Benjamin lives. Near the border of New Hampshire, the town of about 42,670 has deep-rooted ties to the history of the United States. Just over a decade after the Declaration of Independence was signed, Beverly became known as the "birthplace of the American Industrial Revolution" due to the town housing the first cotton mill in America. Townspeople are also adamant that Beverly is the birthplace of the U.S. Navy, although another Massachusetts town, Marblehead, lays claim to the same thing.

It's a town that's eluded the folklore of its neighbor, Salem, home to the infamous witch trials of 1692 and 1693.

As development occurred, Beverly held on closely to its history, but it also seamlessly developed into a breathtaking landscape of parks and bays. Community events fill many summer weekends before days are replaced by frigid winters and Nor'easters. On those warm weekend days, Tim can often be found cruising around in the bays on his boat bearing the words "Life In The Gutter" on the stern, a playful nod to his Reynolds Gutter company.

While Beverly doesn't qualify as a "small town" based on population, it acts like one. People look out for their neighbors, and everyone can be in everyone else's business, for better or worse.

For about 10 years, Tim and Ronnie Benjamin would often escape their idyllic town and head to nearby Middleton to meet at Ferncroft County Club, where they're both club members, to bitch about the Red Sox, taxes or talk about their golf games. The two knew of each other as youngsters, having both grown up in northeast Massachusetts, but a nine-year age gap prevented them from being close. As adults, however, the men bonded and confided in each other as part of the same golf group. They aren't fiercely tight friends but are more than acquaintances.

Ron's golf appearances were becoming less frequent due to his cancer and chemo, of which his golf buddies were aware, as they are all in a highly active text message group. Still, even his golf group didn't know to what extent Ron's health was deteriorating.

Tim would sometimes speak about Ron's devastating cancer diagnosis with his girlfriend, Jessica.

In early October 2023, The Four66 Pub & Grille in the nearby town of Danvers was holding a casual event for the Ferncroft Country Club, which proudly boasts that it has the "North Shore's #1 Finishing Hole." The purpose was for members to draw teams for an upcoming golf tournament. The bar, known for its thin-crust pizzas and barbecue, is what you think of as a locally owned neighborhood pub, filled with sharp-dressed businesspeople, blue-collar workers, shower-deprived souls, sports junkies and families. It carries a bountiful roster of beers and saucy food that guarantees patrons lick their fingers and use plenty of napkins. The townspeople know the ownership family well.

Ronnie has been on a carousel of doctor's visits and fought against attending the benefit despite having gone in previous years. His health story seemed to follow a pattern of one step forward, two steps back, and he didn't want fellow Club members to see him in his current state, fearing he would sadden them or, even worse, be treated differently. Still, something in him told him to go.

After arriving at Four66, Ron gazed at the industrial brick wall behind the bar. Beer taps were busy filling mugs to the brim and the Boston Bruins were playing a preseason game on the plasma TVs affixed to the wall. He soon focused on a long table where about 20 guys were sitting. There was one woman there, too.

He had never before seen this beautiful blond woman drinking Coors Light, but Ron knew almost all the guys, including Tim.

"Ronnie!" Tim called out, happy to see his pal for the first time in almost a year, knowing it wasn't an easy decision to come out. "Come here," Tim continued, "I want you to meet Jess."

Shuffling over to the lone woman, Ron leaned toward her and wrapped his arms around Jessica's shoulders without warning or hesitation. Having never met Ron, Jessica didn't know who this man behind her was, but that hug was tight and meaningful, as if it were between two lifelong friends.

"How you doing? What are you doing with this knucklehead? What's with this?" Ron humorously joked, not giving Jess any chance to respond to the rapid-fire questions.

Given that this guy immediately started busting Tim's balls without any inkling of Jessica's personality, she liked Ron immediately. The two instantly hit it off, and for a brief moment, Ron forgot about the literal death sentence he had been given earlier that same day.

For the first hour of the benefit, Ron beamed when talking about Amy, and there was immense pride in his voice and words when discussing his kids. The elephant in the room, that death sentence, would be addressed later as the crowd diminished.

"How's everything going?" Tim said, concerned, as the evening wore on. By now, the trio of Ronnie, Tim and Jessica were in their own little silo.

"Amy and I found out today that the only way I can live is if we find a liver donor."

Without the donor, Ron likely had less than a year to live.

"So sorries" and oh my God" statements were exchanged. Why was life so cruel to this wonderfully engaging family man?

Tim and Jessica let the news sink in, but their silence was about as loud as the Oasis song playing overhead. Ron nodded, shrugged, and lifted a beer mug to his lips.

"I know you can donate a kidney, but you can actually donate a liver?" Jessica wondered, a hockey jersey for former NHL defenseman Brian Leetch hanging on the wall behind her.

"Yes," Ron nodded.

Liver donations, in general, aren't entirely rare, and they're incredibly safe. They don't get the attention kidney transplants are afforded, but they're no less noble. The first live liver transplant was successfully completed in 1989. In 2021, 9,234 liver transplants were performed in the United States, according to the Department of Health and Human Services, but only about 6% of those were from living donors. Every year, more than 12,000 people join the waiting list for a liver transplant, but conservative estimates indicate that 1,700 people die annually while waiting for a deceased donor. If someone had a living donor who checked off all the qualifications, they could bypass the waitlist and get surgery scheduled.

A living donor with an O-positive blood type was what Ron needed. He couldn't wait.

Enamored by Ron's positive outlook despite the awful hand he'd been dealt, Jessica pondered. She and her family had been through some devastating shit of their own and was helped by the generosity of strangers. When her dad died, she couldn't go a few feet without hearing from a well-wisher asking how they could assist. She always wanted to find a unique way to repay that generosity, but she could never find her "thing." This was her thing. She knew it in her soul and knew her blood type was O-positive.

"I'm going for it," she told Ronnie at the table that night.

"Listen, I appreciate it, I really do," he said, not getting his hopes up, "but this is a big decision. Talk to your family."

Stubborn, Jessica responded, "You have three boys. I have two boys. If nobody helps, they're going to lose their dad. Yesterday was Oct. 1, and it was the anniversary of my dad's death. I was 30 when my dad died, and it sucks. I don't want that for them."

Jessica was indeed 30 when her dad died. Her dad is Kurt von Tillow. Jessica is Mary Jo's daughter.

Had Kurt not passed in the manner that he did, Jessica would likely have never considered donating an organ, especially while alive.

October 2023

Tim and Mary Jo were firmly against Jessica's plan to donate her liver. They felt for Ronnie, Amy and their boys, but donating a liver felt like a bridge too far. Jessica didn't even know Ron, having only met him once that night at the bar.

"I've finally found you. What if you die?" Tim protested. "You're not doing this. I know he's my friend and I love the guy, but you can't do this. You've only known the guy for a few weeks."

"I know," she argued while leaning on the granite kitchen counter of Tim's house, "but if you saw all the things that people did for me and my family with what happened to my dad, you would understand."

"I do understand. I understand you're an amazing person who's willing to do this. It's just I'm being selfish, and I don't want to fucking lose you. I love Ronnie. He's the greatest guy. It has nothing to do with him. It's about you."

Tim, who was fighting back tears, feared that his love story would end with Jessica dying on the surgical table from complications.

Sensing the hurt and terror in Tim's voice, Jessica tenderly walked to him. She affectionately leaned her head on his chest, delicately rubbed his arm and looked up at him.

"That's very sweet, babe," she said. "Nothing's going to happen to me. I'm going to be fine. This guy needs me, and there's nobody else who's going to be able to do it. It's going to be me."

Tim knew about his girlfriend's determination, one of the many things he loves about her, but he was an absolute puddle of emotion as she explained her reasoning.

"After my dad died, people we didn't know were helping us. My mom found comfort in giving talks and speeches at conventions and seminars. A lot of people were doing things like that, but that's not me. That wasn't my thing. This is it."

Jessica was doing this not for her dad but because of him.

Something about Ron reminded Jessica of her dad. Like Kurt, Ronnie is a guy's guy who's very secure with himself, someone who would give the shirt off his back to someone in need. Jessica's young children were forced to grow up without their grandfather, and she wasn't about to see these boys grow up without a dad. When Jessica heard about Ron's situation, it was as if a deafening bell went off in her mind, and she wasn't going to unring it.

Unbeknownst to Ron, behind-the-scenes negotiating had been going on for months. Mary Jo lost count of how many times she attempted to talk Jessica out of it, but knew her arguments might fall on deaf ears—when Jessica makes up her mind about something, good luck trying to persuade her otherwise.

Still, Mary Jo knew her daughter didn't make the decision hastily. She listened to her mom and boyfriend make their cases and agreed with most of what they preached, but she was unmoved. She was going to do this, full stop.

Tim has many close friends that Jessica is close to, but she would never give them a musical organ, let alone a body part. Something about Ron called to Jess. She was aware of his hardships and realized he was a man trying to do right by his family.

Jessica trod lightly when telling her mom of her intentions, knowing it would be a sensitive subject given that Mary Jo spent years rebuilding her collapsed world because of the Vegas shooting in 2017.

"I didn't want to lose her. I wasn't sure I could survive that," Mary Jo said.

As a 15-year-old, Jessica was rendered unconscious at a basketball game after her head snapped back on the hardwood floor during a battle for the ball. Diagnosed with a severe concussion and cracked sternum, she was taken out of the gym on a stretcher, put in the back of an ambulance and transported to the hospital. Her mother prayed the whole time, dreading the worst.

Jessica is a survivor, but not just of the Vegas shooting. During labor with her first son, Carter, the doctor inserted a probe to monitor her contractions and severed the umbilical cord, something that happens in one in every five million pregnancies. The monitors lit up and started screaming as it showed her blood pressure dropping and her baby flatlining.

Doctors immediately whisked her away and performed an emergency C-section to save the lives of her and her baby.

When hearing about the liver donation, Mary Jo had vivid flashbacks of running into the delivery room of Folsom Hospital as "code blue" — a medical emergency — was being called out over the intercom.

Once Carter made his way into the world, he was placed in a cooling bed to prevent further brain damage and taken to UC Davis Medical Center, as its team was more equipped to handle the situation. To make matters worse, Jessica was still recovering at Folsom Hospital and could only see her child via FaceTime for the first three days.

The von Tillows were told that the newborn might have severe brain damage or cerebral palsy, but neither occurred. Not only did Carter survive, but he also had no side effects from the traumatic birth. He is now a bright, athletic, sweet and devilishly handsome kid.

"He's our miracle child," his proud grandma says.

A small sign inside Jessica's Connecticut home reads, "Miracles happen every day," referencing the birth saga.

With her mind harkening back to that intense day in the hospital, Mary Jo immediately and adamantly rejected the idea of a liver donation, fearing Jessica was putting her life in danger.

No matter, Jessica was doing this, knowing her father would be proud of her sacrifice.

As the calendar flipped to 2024, Jessica began undergoing four months of testing to determine if she could even donate her liver and meet the qualifications. She was tested for everything, from diabetes to high blood pressure to allergies. No stone was left unturned. She even did a complete psychiatric evaluation. As a family, the von Tillows and Tim dove deep into liver transplant facts and discovered that Jessica's liver would regenerate to its full pre-donation size in just a few months, and Ron's would grow to full size, too.

It's a tragedy that live liver donations aren't more commonly spoken about.

As Tim watched the whole process unfold and got to know the doctors, he softened his stance and soon applauded Jessica for her brave decision. Mary Jo took more convincing, but she was getting there.

The medical teams candidly spoke about the risks associated with transplants, infection being the most common. Yes, death can happen, doctors admitted, but it's almost a statistical impossibility. For Jess, it was a relatively low-risk surgery that could save a man's life and allow him to skip that lugubrious waitlist.

As no medical facilities performed live liver transplants in Boston, Ron and Jessica were told about a few doctors in Rochester, New York, who had perfected them: Roberto Hernandez Alejandro and Koji Tomiyama.

To no surprise, Jessica, Tim, Amy and Ron researched the doctors and found out that they were the cream of the crop when it came to this type of thing, as they've combined to publish over 150 peer-reviewed publications on the topic.

On March 23, 2024, Jess was officially approved to give 69.5% of her liver to Ronnie. The surgery was set to take place at the University of Rochester Medical Center in Rochester, New York.

Mary Jo booked a flight to the East Coast to be with Jessica and care for her two grandchildren.

April 8, 2024

On the eve of the big day, Jessica and Tim met Ron and Amy for one last pre-surgery meal at The Distillery in Rochester, a simple sports bar with a perpetual array of high-caloric food. The foursome arrived before the crowds descended on the bar to watch the NCAA National Championship basketball game between UConn and Purdue. Over a basket of buffalo wings, the squad talked not just about the surgery but also about the solar eclipse that day. Rochester was one of the areas that saw total darkness for several minutes when the moon passed between the sun and Earth, casting the moon's shadow on the planet.

"How are the boys holding up?" Jess asked Amy.

"Good. They're ready for their dad to be healthy again." She added," How are your boys?"

"Nervous, but fine. My mom is with them."

Unsurprisingly, the conversations eventually turned emotional, and Tim and Amy fought back tears the whole dinner.

"Can you two hold it together?" an annoyed Jessica asked, not mincing words.

Ron, who was literally living on borrowed time, just laughed. Deep down, though, he was reflective and appreciative of the moment. He had been told his surgery would last nearly an entire day.

"I just want to wake up the next day," he kept saying. It was his mantra.

Twelve hours later, things got real.

April 9, 2024

When they all arrived at the hospital waiting room at 5:30 a.m., the mood was understandably solemn. Everyone within eyesight was either giving an organ, receiving an organ, or supporting someone involved in organ transplanting. With a pall of nervousness hanging in the air, a local news broadcast played on a small TV in the corner of the room. Several people milled around the small coffee pot serving jet-black sludge.

The vinyl chairs were as uncomfortable as the energy.

"Hey buddy, do you have a coffee cup?" Ron asked a fellow future transplant recipient.

"Yeah, right here," the man said, handing over an empty Dixie cup.

"OK," Ron boomed loudly, gripping the small paper cup in his hand. "Everyone put in five bucks in the cup. Whoever gets the biggest transplant today gets the pool money. If you get two things transplanted, you win."

The tension in the room was broken. Amy shook her head, knowing that her husband was already returning to form before the surgery.

"Kidney transplant people, you're out," Ron declared. "A heart transplant is a contender. Liver might be a winner."

Ron's standup act was crushing but short-lived after a nurse called his name. He looked at Amy and breathed deeply. They locked eyes. Impenetrable.

As they hugged, he turned his head into her ear.

"This is it. I love you. Just let me wake up tomorrow."

"I love you."

Jessica's name was called simultaneously, and the liver duo followed the nurse through the door of the UR Medicine Kidney, Pancreas, and Liver Transplant Institute. It was only a couple of seconds, but time stood still. For the next 90 minutes, Jessica sat in a curtained-off, petite-sized nook as doctors tested Ron in a nearby room to make sure the cancer hadn't spread and that his body was strong enough to take a liver. Realistically, doctors were determining if Ron was going to get surgery or die. If the cancer had spread, death was all but inevitable, as the transplant would be canceled.

"Jessica," a nurse said at 7 a.m. "We're ready for you."

The fact that Jessica was being called meant that everything checked out. Tim, who'd been allowed to join his girlfriend in that antiseptic curtained-off alcove where she'd been waiting, started sweating, and his heart pounded like a jackhammer, knowing that his girlfriend of three years was destined for the operating table.

There was no turning back.

For nine hours, Jessica was put under while Dr. Hernandez Alejandro removed the majority of her healthy (sometimes beer-soaked) liver. Ronnie was out for 18 hours while Dr. Tomiyama worked on him.

Knowing there was nothing they could do, Tim and Amy tried to take their minds off the surgeries over breakfast at the Cracker Barrel, but that was like asking a fish to stop swimming—all they could do was cry and talk about the situation. Tissues were in high demand at their table as both blubbered through their thoughts. They didn't bother to hide their emotions as the waitress placed biscuits on the table.

"They're going to be fine," Tim kept saying as the aroma of sweet waffles and bacon stimulated their senses. "This is going to be a blip on your radar. We're going to get through this, and you guys are going to live a long life."

It was hard to tell if he believed it through his watering eyes and shaking voice.

While Tim is never shy about telling a joke (even at inopportune times), it was Amy who broke the tension during lunch at another restaurant.

"We're hugging, having deep conversations and crying everywhere we go. Did it ever dawn on you that these people probably think we're a couple divorcing or breaking up?"

While Ron and Jess were under anesthesia, Tim and Amy went to their hotel rooms and took much-needed power naps after lunch. They promised to exchange any updates or information they received.

At around 5 p.m., Tim's phone rang. He recognized the phone number on the caller ID as the hospital. His heart raced, and he couldn't answer fast enough, hoping to hear good news.

"Hi Tim," the nurse on the other end said. "Jessica is awake. You can come see her now."

Knowing that Amy still had nine hours of agony, he felt awful leaving her, but he had to.

"I need to go be with Jess," he said.

"Of course, go, go, go!"

Tim probably could have gotten an Olympic silver medal for how fast he ran through the hospital.

Upon seeing Jess, or at least a shell of her (she was still under all those drugs), Tim sobbed, clasped his hands and praised her bravery. He then reached into his right pants pocket, pulled out his cell phone and tapped out a message to that aforementioned active text message group with his golf buddies.

"Just wanted to give you guys an update, Jess is awake and she's doing great. Ron is still under, but things are going well."

April 10, 2024

In the wee hours of the morning on April 10, Ron's eyelids started flickering slowly. It was pitch black outside, so artificial light filled the sterile hospital room. Donning a blue hospital gown and connected to more tubes than a water park, he began slowly waking up and opening his eyes. Amy, his stunning brunette bride with an infectious smile, was in the room with him. Her eyes sparkled, and relief came over her when Ron's pupils adjusted to his surroundings.

"How's Jess?"

After 18 hours of unconsciousness, those were the first words out of his mouth. He then said, "What day is it?"

"She's good. She's recovering a few rooms away."

"And babe, it's Wednesday," Amy added. "You woke up."

All he wanted to do was "wake up tomorrow." Mission accomplished.

For the next several hours, machines attached to Ronnie beeped and doctors shuffled in and out of the unexceptional hospital room to check his vitals. Ronnie then asked his wife to take a picture of him for Facebook to prove he was alive.

"Ronnie's transplant was a HUGE success! He has asked me to post a photo to show how well he is doing, in hopes it will encourage others to never give up!" Amy penned next to an image of her husband sitting in a recliner, still in that blue hospital gown. After thanking the doctors and the entire transplant team for "truly performing miracles," she wrote. "Jess, Ronnie has a portion of your liver, but you have our heart."

Doctors were naturally cautious with the transplanter and the transplantee, both remaining there for several days. On April 13, Ron's boys brought Jessica a bouquet of mylar balloons filled with helium, one of which was an oversized bear with the message "Get Well Soon" on its tummy. The bear had casts on its right arm and left foot and a bandage over its eye. Since she was on so many painkillers from the surgery, she was prone to hallucinations, and the bear began talking to her at one point.

This delusion was medical grade!

"What's going on?" she asked Tim in a somewhat annoyed tone.

"What do you mean?" he asked while thumbing through a magazine.

"I think I'm hallucinating."

Tim giggled. "Well, what's going on?"

"Well, whose fucking baby is crawling across the ground in the room with us, Tim!"

As a nurse walked in to check on Jessica and the nonexistent baby, Tim piped up, "You got any extra drugs I can have?"

When Jessica was eventually released, she refused to take the balloons with her upon release.

"That bear fucked with me for a week straight," she said, adding, "Those drugs were obviously really good."

What wasn't a hallucination was when the hospital went on lockdown that Saturday after a patient who'd been in police custody escaped.

"The perimeter of the main entrance parking lot is covered with law enforcement. On our drive into this parking lot, police could be seen at every turn," a WROC-TV news correspondent tweeted at the time.

Finger Lakes Daily News reported that an inmate suffered a medical issue while in jail and was taken to the hospital. On April 13, deputies were alerted that he had left the hospital, prompting police to swarm the medical facility. The man was later found at his home and arrested.

On April 16, exactly one week after receiving 69.5% of a new liver, Ronnie walked out of the hospital in a green Boston Celtics shirt and blue Los Angeles Dodgers hat. His beard was extra bushy from not shaving for a week.

While Ron and Jess were also anxious to get home, they experienced post-surgery hiccups and returned to the hospital — he had some infections and was even septic at one point. Meanwhile, she contracted an infection from sneezing and gained weight because her body wasn't processing fluids properly. For a couple of months, the transplanter and the transplantee experienced intolerable pain, but everything soon settled down, leaving both of them with no regrets.

Jessica quite literally saved Ron's life.

Summer 2024

Ron had just arrived home from a long day of slicing and dicing metal at his shop. It had been about four months since he was cut open and bequeathed a portion of Jessica's vital organ. Since then, he and Amy have kept in touch with Jessica. They met up a few times over the summer of 2024 and even took the kids out on the water to tool around the Danvers River and Beverly Channel. While some adults sipped on some cold beer during the boat ride, Ron had refrained, having been told upon receiving Jessica's organ that he could never drink alcohol again.

He hadn't been home long when his phone buzzed from an incoming text message. Looking down at the screen, Ron noticed a message from Jessica. He and Jess have an unwavering friendship, one that consists of constant humorous needling, so he knew what was coming. Ron had heard all the jokes about his liver and colon. In fact, on May 12, seeing that he now has a liver from a female, he was bombarded with "Happy Mother's Day" texts from friends. He took it all in stride and loved the creativity of the lighthearted harassment.

A typical New Englander, Ron can take a razzing and dish it out. When he and Jessica get together, they spend hours attempting to one-up each other by insulting a very game Tim. For all the ball-busting, though, Ron has a sentimental side, and he quite literally wears his heart on his sleeve - his right forearm is tattooed with a series of names and numbers: the word "Amy" sits atop, followed by the initials of his three sons. Under that are the numbers 12-4-61, 8-16-87 and 4-9-24. The last set of numbers is the transplant date; the middle set is Jessica's birthday; the third set is her father Kurt von Tillow's birthday.

"Hey, how's my liver?" Jessica's text message said. "Listen, I'm not advocating for you to go get drunk, but my liver is going to be very upset if you don't drink for the rest of your life."

A few minutes later, Ron walked to the fridge, grabbed a beer and sat on the couch. Gripping the can with his left hand, he flipped the tab up with his right hand and heard that familiar sound of an open aluminum can. He took one drink, letting the hoppy liquid roll around his mouth before swallowing.

"Ahhhhh."

Setting the can down, he grabbed his phone and typed a message to Jessica.

"It tastes so good. Your liver is very happy right now."

March 2025

A massive pile of mail greeted Mary Jo von Tillow after arriving to her Southern California home. Having spent the entire holiday season and then some on the East Coast, traveling between Florida, Connecticut and South Carolina, the letters and junk mail had mounted.

She had been away so long that, in fact, she was just now opening up Christmas cards, and there were a lot of them. As she sat on her L-shaped couch, she came across a red envelope with a return address of Gloucester, Mass. Tim, she knew, lived near there, but she wasn't quite sure who sent this.

Sliding her finger under the back tab, she began opening the festive envelope, believing a Christmas card was inside. After cracking the seal, she reached her hand into the envelope, felt heavy card stock and pulled out its contents.

She beamed upon seeing a photo of Ronnie, Amy and their three boys posing on the beach. Donning a blue dress shirt and light khaki pants, Ron looked healthy. His salt-and-pepper beard was well-kept, and his smile was contagious. The boys all appeared happy and athletic. Amy, the rock of the family, was as pretty as a picture in her white dress. A message on the card read, "What a Wonderful Life. Merry Christmas from the Benjamin Family."

In flipping the card over, Mary Jo saw something different: an image of two people, a man and a woman, bundled up in front of Niagara Falls with the Skylon Tower in the distance. The man in the photo was layered in a black hoodie and a blue and white flannel shirt. A Boston Celtics hat sat atop his head. The woman dressed in a black puffer coat, her blond hair falling pat the lapel ever so gently. There, on the back of the Benjamin family Christmas card, were Jessica and Tim.

The message on the bottom was simple, short and summed up everything for the Benjamins: #thankyoujess.

AUTHORS NOTE

This book would not have been possible without the trust and time of its subjects and everyone else involved, especially my dear friend Mary Jo von Tillow and her incredible family. Over the past few years, MJ and I have spent countless hours together, be it in person, on the phone or even on Zoom. Needless to say, we have developed a deep bond that I cherish, which is clearly a silver lining that stemmed from Oct. 1, 2017. Had that day not happened, and we all wish it hadn't, MJ and I would have never met or come together for this project. Although I've been published probably thousands of times via my work in entertainment journalism, writing for People Magazine, Rolling Stone, Entertainment Weekly and so many others, it's because of her and this project that I'm able to live out my dream to become an author. I'm still unclear why she put so much faith in me, but I'm deeply indebted.

To my loving family who supported me in this endeavor and put up with all my late-night writing, exhausted facial expressions and delayed dinners, especially my extraordinary wife, Kacy, you guys have been unapologetically by my side, and I'm forever grateful. Dad, I wish you could have seen this book; I can only imagine how proud you would be.

A true labor of love, *Tragic Connections* was the result of hundreds of hours of interviews and research. Sometimes, interviews were conducted in person or over the phone

— more often than not, multiple interviews with the same person were required. I'm sure I've annoyed these wonderful people too many times.

I met Mary Jo von Tillow at an Angels baseball game in May 2022. I was on assignment from Rolling Stone to help write a story on the fifth anniversary of Route 91. Once a year, during Country Weekend, survivors of the massacre gather to hang out and root for the Angels. However, no one really pays attention to the game, choosing instead to mingle and laugh and remember their lost family members. In the lead-up to the game, I spoke with Melissa Williams, who organizes the annual event as part of her 58 Strong organization, and she graciously introduced me to people she thought would be great for the story. Although Mary Jo had done many interviews about that night, she seemed somewhat reluctant to speak to me. I was persistent but not pushy throughout the nine innings of the game. We finally talked while standing in line to watch country singer Josh Turner, who was playing on the diamond after the Angels polished off the A's 5-3. "OK, let's go," she told me, waving me over as fireworks shot up into the air to celebrate the home team's win. For the next 15 minutes, she told me about her Route 91 experience, which was undoubtedly horrific. I have heard a lot of stories — all of them worth listening to — but I was moved by her story more so than most.

On Sept. 21, 2022, a story I co-wrote with Jonathan Bernstein was published on Rolling Stone's website with the headline, "Five Years Since the Route 91 Massacre No One Knows a Damn Thing." It was also published in the October 2022 edition of Rolling Stone Magazine — that photo of the broken windows that Matthew Von Tillow saw from his airplane was the lead image.

I honestly didn't think I'd hear from Mary Jo again, but she reached out to me a year later via text message with an idea for this book. She could have certainly asked an accomplished book author to write this book, but there's a reason she reached out to me: I was also there on Oct. 1, 2017, albeit with a different group of people. I actually wrote a first-person account of the shooting (from my perspective) about three hours after the bullets stopped flying. It was posted on RollingStone.com in the early morning hours of Oct. 2, 2017. To this day, I've never read what I wrote, but I hear it's "very raw." As a journalist, I've written well over 10,000 published articles, but that first story was arguably my most-read piece… or so I hear.

That evening, I was on the east side of the venue in a "suite," which was essentially a fancy, refurbished shipping container. It was three levels tall and had windows. It was an upgraded tin can. I was standing just outside of the suite's entryway when the shooting started, so I was among the first to run in and take shelter. While lying on the metal ground, I remember the windows getting shot out and glass shards falling on my back — one person even climbed through the window, and I momentarily thought it might be the shooter. The sound of the gunshots reverberated, making it seem like multiple people were inside carrying out a mass killing. I still don't know how long I was on the ground, but I remember every second of it, and it felt like a lifetime. Our group escaped during a small break in the shooting (presumably when the madman was changing guns and perspectives). In my exit from the festival grounds, it was clear to see that people were wounded and dead. "Where's the fucking hospital!" someone in a pickup shouted as I was leaving the venue. Like others, I hopped a fence and headed toward the Las Vegas airport, which was close. Upon seeing a line of semis in a barren field, I got behind those. Several people had the same idea, and they got behind the trucks (rather fitting since Kurt was a truck driver, and I felt safest behind those trucks). I don't know when it happened, but after a while, hunkered down in the dirt behind the semi-trailer, I realized the shooting had stopped.

Although I live in Las Vegas, it took hours to get home, as all roads around the venue had been cordoned off. Once I got home, I made some requisite phone calls to family and started writing. I didn't read what I wrote before hitting "send" and shipping it off to Rolling Stone.

Upon seeing what I had filed and reading the horror I'd experienced, my Nashville-based editor Joe Hudak replied in an email, "Oh my God. Mark. Oh my God. I'm so sorry." There are war correspondents who have seen fewer. Once the story was published, it was just a matter of minutes before media outlets wanted to speak to me. I turned almost all of them down, but I did talk to People magazine since they gave me my start in magazine writing. I'm forever indebted to them.

The evening had a significant impact on me and all of us, and all for different reasons. When Mary Jo first approached me about this book, I was flattered and terrified. Neither of us knew what would come of it or how open people would be, but the Von Tillow family took me as if I were one of their own. On a warm August Sunday in 2023, I flew to Orange County to meet with Mary Jo in her quaint apartment just a few blocks from the ocean. While surrounded by beachfront homes and overlooking Spanish-style roofs discolored by the sun, we sat for hours swapping our Route 91 stories in exact and excruciating detail. She seems as interested in my story as I was in hers. Mary Jo believes that Kurt may have been the first person fatally shot that evening. There's a good chance that's true. I believe the first person shot, albeit not fatally, was near me. At the time, I thought the screaming woman had been hit with a firework, maybe a bottle rocket.

By now, it's probably fair to say that every person at the festival that night has a canned story that they can tell in their sleep, as we've all recounted the tale so many times — not to be flippant about the situation, but it's our dark, perverse party trick in a way. During that initial California afternoon at Mary Jo's home, she and I didn't just recount our differing experiences on that fateful night, but we also spoke about life in general. She rarely went a few minutes without smiling or bringing up Kurt, Matthew or Jessica.

Because Jessica was there that day, the mother-daughter bond they share is indescribable — Mary Jo has leaned on her so much since that day that I'm honestly surprised she hasn't toppled over.

"We've definitely got closer, and this is not to say we weren't close before, but you kind of hinge any boundaries that were there," Jessica told me. "I will say the thing that has changed the most is that my mom keeps evolving. She has evolved into exactly who she needs to be, who she should be and where she wants to be in life. That's what my dad would have wanted for her. She's made her life really great for how shitty she could be."

Matthew, who now lives in South Carolina, sees his mom as an "anchor" for many people. "There was a lot of emptiness and a lot of hard times for her, and there still are. We all probably think about my dad every day, and it's all mostly positive things, but there's still an emptiness in there with her. How do you fill that void of loving and being hurt, but that's what she tries to do," he says.

While preparing for this book, my initial meeting with Mary Jo was tentatively planned for the previous day. Still, I had to stay in Las Vegas to interview *Real Housewives* star Erika Girardi for my day job with People Magazine. When I told Mary Jo this, she laughed. Ironically, the *Housewives* star had a part in Mary Jo's story in a roundabout way — Erika's estranged husband, Tom Girardi, was involved in Mary Jo's lawsuit with MGM for the shooting. Following the shooting, many victims, widows and attendees filed a lawsuit against MGM, as Mandalay Bay and the festival grounds were both owned by the casino giant. In the class action lawsuit with 4,400 victims, MGM was accused of negligence, wrongful death and liability. In the end, the casino company settled for $800 million. Mary Jo and many others used Tom Girardi's law firm to represent them. In 2020, Tom had legal issues of his own after he was accused of embezzling money from the victims of Lion Air Flight 610, which crashed into the western Pacific Ocean in 2018 during a flight from Jakarta, Indonesia, to Pangkal Pinang, Indonesia. All 189 passengers and crew died. Around the same time the MGM settlement was happening, Tom Girardi was disbarred, and his law firm, Girardi & Keese, filed for bankruptcy. Luckily for Mary Jo and her family, another law firm was involved and stepped in to clean up the mess.

"We had to go through a bankruptcy trustee to issue our settlement, even though it was rightfully ours. It was still part of the bankruptcy of Girardi & Keese," she said.

I find Mary Jo to be a remarkable woman, a vibrant woman who seems equally at ease at home as she does in large gatherings. She could have folded up her chair, retreated and been sorrowful forever. Traveling certainly helped her mental state, as did meeting people like Tommy Maher, Jeff Dion and others.

In the early days after the shooting, Matthew and Jessica were not wholly supportive of their mom's newfound openness to, well, strangers. Jessica, who works for a software company in Connecticut, feared that her mom was becoming the "face" of Route 91 victims because she was granting so many media interviews (including mine, albeit five years later).

"To me, that wasn't who my mom is," Jessica said. "I'd get mad at her for all the fucking people she involves herself in her life."

Matthew is aware that his bond with his mother is different than the one Jessica has, as he wasn't there in Las Vegas that night.

"They had to survive somebody shooting them, and the whole group that they were with definitely has that connection. That's something that I'll never have, but I don't regret it," he says. "I don't look back and feel like, 'Man, I should have been there.' It's not something that drives me or gives me any kind of regret or emotion. It's just a fact of a traumatic situation. Their relationship definitely changed that night and forever on."

Knowing what Mary Jo has endured, Jill Carson "marvels" at her older sister.

"She's a strong, strong woman, always been strong, independent," Jill said. "Coming from our family, we had to be a little bit independent financially if we wanted things, but her strength really came from Kurt. He didn't like negativity. He didn't want to be around people who were negative or not fun. He was very positive, and I think she kind of knew that he would not want her to not move on with her life, not go out and do things. He would not want her to be depressed and lie in bed and be sad for him."

As we set out on this book together, we both wanted it to be honest. I told her that Kurt seemed like an incredible man, a dedicated father and a loyal husband. I also told her he was no saint because no one is. She agreed. In the years after Kurt's death, Mary Jo wasn't desperate to find love again, but she dated and had serious relationships, but wasn't quite ready. She even had a long-distance relationship with a man in Vancouver, which ended shortly after the 2020/2021 COVID pandemic. She's since found a wonderful man in Florida who is kind, caring, loving, empathetic and not intimidated by her past. She sees a real chance at loving again for the first time since Kurt's passing.

Neither Matthew nor Jessica has a problem with their mother dating. They're both rational. Still, their mother said dating was "horrible" — not because she's comparing every man to her late husband, but because, well, dating *is* horrible. Having loved and lost, she expected dating to be carefree. She yearned for a man without chaos in his life, someone without baggage. I felt comfortable when I bluntly told her, "Maybe men see you as having baggage, too." I remember the moment vividly, sitting on her couch as ocean air attempted to cool the room via the open windows. I didn't know how she'd take my comment.

"You're right," she conceded. "I have a lot of baggage, and a lot of guys would be scared away by that, and that's ok."

Mary Jo is scarred and self-aware for the most part.

In speaking to Matthew for the very first time, I brought up his mother's notion that she feels she "got the best version" of Kurt, but he "never got the best version" of her. Matthew quickly dismissed it. "Yeah, I think that's a cute thing to say," he told me. "I think my dad, if he was here, would say he's lucky as hell to have somebody like my mom."

Mary Jo's inner circle, some of whom are documented in this book, are lucky as hell to have her, too.

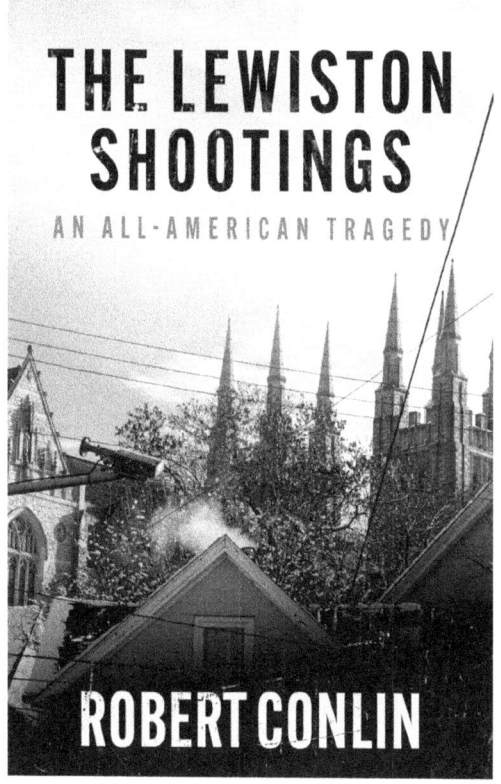

www.ingramcontent.com/pod-product-compliance
Lightning Source LLC
Chambersburg PA
CBHW061728120626
46550CB00005B/1746